The Suspect in Poetry

THE SUSPECT IN POETRY

by

JAMES DICKEY

1964

THE SIXTIES PRESS

For permission to reprint, the author is grateful to *Poetry,
The Sewanee Review, The Hudson Review, The New York
Times Book Review,* and *The Virginia Quarterly Review,* in
which some of these essays and reviews have appeared.

Library of Congress Catalogue Card Number
62 — 21968

Printed in the Republic of Ireland

CONTENTS

THE SUSPECT IN POETRY

THE SUSPECT IN POETRY

AT one time or another, and perhaps at most times, the long-term reader of poetry must marvel at the hundreds and hundreds of lines, stanzas, themes, and whole poems which seem to be sheer effrontery to his sense of what the truth of their subjects must be or could possibly be : that seem to have been invented to satisfy the rules of some complicated but learnable (for many have learned) game which keeps changing from generation to generation, but which always, whether it means to or not, brings into being a truly remarkable amount of utter humbug, absolutely and uselessly far-fetched and complex manipulation of language. The touch upon words of a humanly perceived beauty, terror, or mystery is rare indeed, for a fundamental kind of unliterary innocence is necessary in a writer before he can undergo these feelings. They cannot be expressed out of nothing but good will and the current fashions of an art. For all readers, then, almost all poetry contains elements that are suspect, having no relation to what the readers believe in as "reality," and even in a sense degrading it by offering experience as a series of unbelievable contrivances, none of which has the power of bringing forth a genuine response. Oddly enough, it is only in poems wherein we forget that our feelings have been deliberately evoked that poetry as an art justifies itself. One thing is certain; if the reader does not, through the writing, gain a new, intimate, and vital perspective on his own life as a human being, there is no poem at all, or only a poem written by a collective entity called "Modern Poetry, Period 1945-1960." What makes the whole thing difficult, of course, is that what may be suspect to me may well be genuine to you, and consequently we enter into a thorough critical chaos.

This is, I suspect, where we should be, anyway. What matters is that there be some real response to poems, some passionate and private feeling about them: that for certain people there be certain poems that speak directly to them as they believe God would. And it is hard to regard most of the poems we read in this light. Most of our contemporary poets are writing out into a Climate of poetic officialdom, or pre-tested Approval, based largely on the principles which the New Criticism has espoused, and on the opinions of those who Count in modern letters. We have lost all sense of personal intimacy between the poet and his reader, and even between the poet and his non-poetical self, the self that eats, walks down the street, fills out forms, pays taxes, not as a poet, but in the same ways everybody else does. A very real invasion of privacy has taken place and turned the poet into a kind of monster whose very efforts to appear human, forgiving, compassionate, and lovable must be looked upon with suspicion, as just so many devices, comparable to the brochures used by salesmen or the broadcasts of the Voice of America. Because he knows with Eliot that art is autotelic, he also knows a great deal of what there is to know about evoking, by means of the craft of verse, selected emotions in his readers. For this reason, everything he does comes to seem a manipulation, much in the same way that advertising or any other propaganda is. This air of falseness, of the Suspect in poetry, is one cause of the fatal and much-deplored rift between poet and audience in our time. Very subtly, the feeling of basic honesty, of emotional honesty (but what, exactly, is that?) has evaporated from our poetry; there is no longer a sense of communion involved: that communion upon which all meaningful communication in the arts depends. " The poets lie too much " has grown from a still small voice into a thundering accusation,

10

though it has been with us at least since Plato. When we sit down to a book of poems, to a poem, we need to get back to something as simple as Norman Douglas's " What has this fellow got to say to *me*? " I don't wish to blink the question of form and content, with which I have no ability to contend, anyway: only to point out some of the reasons we don't really experience poetry any more, but only judge it. And therefore care little about it except as the fodder necessary to nourish our literary opinions. And that is too bad. Too bad for poetry, certainly, but worst of all for us.

THE WINTERS APPROACH

I—DONALD DRUMMOND

Donald F. Drummond is a writer whom I have watched for several years with some admiration, but with more dismay and regret. That he is one of the best of a generation of the pupils of Yvor Winters I have no doubt at all. His poems, thoughtful, cleanly conceived and executed, and displaying almost a control-beyond-control of their material, have a great deal of compression, intelligence, and wit. Yet he seems to me a completely unsatisfactory poet. In common with almost all other Winters-trained writers, Drummond appears to have assimilated entirely, and to have put to extremely effective use, the well-known principles and techniques upon which Winters insists with his characteristic air of finality. This enables Drummond to operate with a certain measure of success within disastrously narrow bounds, and cuts him off entirely from writing poems of permanent value. Worse; one often has the feeling that Mr. Drummond is not a poet at all, in the Platonic sense, but is by choice a kind of minor artisan in words, who has learned all he can from his guild-master, and is unwilling or unable to contribute anything of his own beyond. Many of the pieces in *The Battlement* are quite obviously (to use a phrase of F. R. Leavis) no more than "occasions for the exercise of the verse craft." Drummond writes

> Excess of light, prohibited
> By the double-rayed diffusive terms
> At source and sorcerer, becomes
> The mystery which is scarletness

Seen in its whole, the violent red
Of quick, aerated blood, arterial
And central near the body's heart.

When one determines from the rest of the poem that
this elaborate passage, involving human eyes seen as
burning-glasses, a " mystery," and the color of the blood
as it leaves the heart, is simply an overingenious trope
meant to define the color of a woman's dress, it is hard
to suppress an unbelieving smile at the wasted seriousness
and effort which concocted it; it is even more difficult to
avoid a certain amount of impatience regarding a system
of values that would reduce the rich, multiple excess of
the imagination to the bare, starved, and creatureless
bones strewn through this book and some of the others
like it which Alan Swallow makes available to us.

In spite of their admirable concision, all of Drummond's
poems are denatured, dry, and in their lack of physical
concreteness strike me as being no refutation at all to
William James' belief that " the deeper features of reality
are found only in perceptual experience." Rather than a
refining and "understanding " of experience, a kind of
calculated bleaching-process has taken place, wherein
life is reduced to a colorless abstraction of itself. The
body does not, for example, hurt, but " suffers indignity."
Something " portends " something else, so that a third
thing may "misinterpret where it apprehends." And
so on. The result of Drummond's practise: his carefully-
staged conceits, his logical-as-a-time-table metaphors, his
merciless regularity of accent, is not the massive sense
and depth of inevitability and rightness of the great
practitioners of the strict forms (Dryden, Yeats, Valéry),
but neatness merely: tidiness: the wrapping up of a
small ordinary parcel with habitual skill and dispatch.

13

I cannot, however, for the life of me get rid of the notion that Drummond is a larger poet than he has yet appeared to be. The release of this poet (if he exists) from the stone, will, of course, have to be effected by Drummond himself. I should like to see him lose himself for a year or so in the huge variety of Shakespeare, read modern continental verse, even wade shamelessly about in sentimentality. A glacial and sanctioned " purity " of the sort displayed in *The Battlement* has but little chance of contributing anything of value to either the language or the human beings who use it. In a few shocking, rebellious fragments in his book, Drummond appears to possess more individuality and insight than any of the other poets of his persuasion I have read; I would, if I could, enlist him on the side of humanity, rather than that of the Angels, whatever desperate remedies were required.

The Battlement, by Donald Drummond, Alan Swallow, 1956. $2.50

II—ELLEN KAY

Ellen Kay is a tractable student of the Wintersian virtues, and seems to take as axiomatic that learning to concoct acceptable little quasi-philosophical proposition-making verses that scan constitutes all that one can hope to achieve in the way of human expression. One sees immediately that nature is never itself in Miss Kay's poems; nor does it belong to Miss Kay in any intimate and revealing connection. It belongs to the Proposition which it may be made to yield, if the poet rigs a satis-factory set of syllogisms. For this kind of writing, the myths do as well as (or perhaps better than) things seen and known; consequently there are poems on Pluto and Ceres, Eve, the unicorn, Tiresias, The Living Narcissus,

14

and, no less wonderful in the pantheon of West-coast neo-classicism, One Intent upon the Doctorate. Perhaps this is all just as well, for Miss Kay's powers of observation are decidedly slight. But when one sees, also, that her ability to make decisive generalizations is not much above that of the average graduate student, one becomes restive. She says that a stone found in the sea is "licked small and smooth by rough/Tongues of wave, in beauty/ Its own cosmography . . ." Isn't this a kind of predictable dressing-up of a poetic commonplace? What more haggard cliché could the poet have come upon than waves seen as tongues, albeit rough ? I find this going-a-platitude-one-better occurring so frequently throughout Miss Kay's book that it has all the appearance of being systematized, and I can't, despite my best efforts, escape the conclusion that Miss Kay is an almost frightening example of all the worst faults, quickly acquired, and middling virtues, come by somewhat more slowly (but I should think not much) of the average Winters-trained poet, primly preaching a set of academic homilies (" the mind is . . . " " lust is . . ." " love is not . . ." etc.), wherein painfully-contrived arguments in rhyme substitute for genuine insight, and the whole is delivered in diction like nothing ever spoken in truth or understandable error : " Comfort cannot insure./Life is no sinecure . . ." or (my personal favourite), " April holds their last breath;/ Catabolic law, guiled/By the mind's strategy,/Moves to finality/Without return." In the end one reads this kind of writing only as another more serious-minded and semi-codified form of jargon verse; in any meaningful sense it is subjectless, all " strategy " and no passion, all will-power and no luck.

A *Local Habitation,* by Ellen Kay, Alan Swallow, 1958, $2.00.

ALLEN GINSBERG

I—*Howl*

I admit, as anyone must, that my own sensibility may exhibit terrible failures of eye, ear, mind, and nerve. Such an admission has grave consequences, and a good many of the terrors of responsibility. Because of my own defects of taste, I fear, for example, that I may diminish some perfectly respectable reader's pleasure in the work of Allen Ginsberg, who has written the following lines.

> What sphinx of cement and aluminum bashed open their
> skulls and ate up their brains and imagination?
> Moloch! Solitude! Filth! Ugliness! Ashcans and un-
> obtainable dollars! Children screaming under the
> stairways! Boys sobbing in armies! Old men
> weeping in the parks!

It is at least theoretically possible that I may do a certain amount of harm, also, to the celebrated " Bay Area Renaissance " if I say, with a tone of condescension I don't like but find myself using anyway, that Ginsberg's writings are of the familiar our-love-against-their-machines-and-money variety, strongly akin to those of Henry Miller, Kenneth Patchen, and Kenneth Rexroth, but lacking entirely the memorable and individual qualities of these: Miller's surrealist sexual humor, Patchen's occasional beauties of imagery, and Rexroth's serious and moving contemplation of Time. There are some chances one must take, however; among contemporary poets, Ginsberg is the perfect inhabitant, if not the very founder of Babel, where conditions do not so much make tongues incomprehensible, but render their utterances, as poetry, meaningless. *Howl* is the skin of Rimbaud's *Une Saison en Enfer* thrown over the conventional maunderings of

16

one type of American adolescent, who has discovered that machine civilization has no interest in his having read Blake. The pattern of introduction of works of this type is familiar : they are offered as " confession," with the warning (here by William Carlos Williams) that their authors have indeed " descended into Hell " and come back with a marvellous and terrible Truth to tell us, all about ourselves and the world we have made. The principal state of mind is thus hallucination; everyone in Ginsberg's book is hopped-up on benzedrine, reefers, or whiskey, and is doing something as violently and loudly as he can, in " protest " or " fulfillment." What emerges from all this is an Attitude, since most of the writing itself is in no sense distinctive. The Attitude, however, is really not worth examining either, since Ginsberg's idea of " revolt " seems essentially to consist in making of oneself " cocksman and Adonis of Denver."

If I pay Ginsberg more attention than he perhaps merits, I do so because I have long harbored what now seems to be a rather frightening assumption: that among the unschooled, self-educated, brash, and relatively manner-less poets whose books are issued by small publishers like " The City Lights Bookshop," there might one day appear a writer to supply the in-touch-with-living authenticity which current American poetry so badly needs, grown as it has genteel and almost suffocatingly proper. *Howl* is certainly not the work I have been awaiting. And yet, and yet . . . Having established Ginsberg in (or as) Babel, is one, then, utterly sure that in this estimate some important things have not been left out ? Isn't it true of his work, for instance, that somewhere amongst its exhibitionist welter of unrelated associations, wish-fulfillment fantasies, and self-righteous maudlinness, a confused but believable passion for values is struggling ? Are there not a few indiscriminately

17

scattered passages which indeed do have upon them a good deal of the constricted, screaming fury Ginsberg feels against his world ? And is it quite fair to say that he lacks *entirely* the better qualities of his literary kin : Patchen, Miller, and Rexroth ? Is not, say, his description of the baggage racks in " In the Baggage Room at Greyhound " one of the funniest and most horrifying catalogues (and typical baggage racks) in contemporary writing ?

> It was the racks, I realized, sitting myself on top of
>   them now as is my wont at lunchtime to rest my
>   tired foot,
> it was the racks, great wooden shelves and stanchions
>   posts and beams assembled floor to roof jumbled
>   with baggage,
> —the Japanese white metal postwar trunk gaudily
>   flowered and headed for Fort Bragg,
> one Mexican green paper package in purple rope
>   adorned with names for Nogales,
> hundreds of radiators all at once for Eureka,
> crates of Hawaiian underwear,
> rolls of posters scattered over the Peninsula, nuts to
>   Sacramento,
> one human eye for Napa,
> an aluminum box of human blood for Stockton
> and a little red package of human teeth for Calistoga—

No; I must admit that the comic talent that noted and collected these items seems to me considerable. And if a measure of craft were to be exercised ? What then ? It is hardly fair to hope that Ginsberg will ever come to agree with himself that this is necessary, but I for one will buy and read what he writes, should he do so.

Howl, by Allen Ginsberg, City Lights Books, 1956, $.75.

II—*Kaddish*

It is fun to imagine the exhilaration that must seize people who "always thought they might be poets" when they try the Allen Ginsberg method and find out that, after all, they *are* poets. In each case the needed equipment is very simple : a life, with its memories, frustrations, secret wishes (very important, these !), an ability to write elementary prose and to supply it with rather more exclamation points than might normally be called for; these show transport, awe, horror and other important emotions.

Later, refinements may be introduced, such as Zen Buddhism and the frequent use of words like " strange," " mad," " tragic," " visionary," " angelic," " apocalyptic " —and lo ! the neophyte is revealed as a full-blown Ginsbergian or beatnik poet, qualified to read in coffee houses, wear a beard and serve as a " living symbol " of protest and freedom.

Mr. Ginsberg's new poems in *Kaddish*, like his old poems, seem not so much themselves as a convenient prototype of all such writing : a strewn, mishmash prose consisting mainly of assertions that its author is possessed, is often if not always in " holy ecstasy," and so on. But the writing belies all such claims quite heartlessly; there is nothing holy about it in any sense that I can understand, and its obsession is evidenced only by its efforts to be so. Confession is not enough, and neither is the assumption that the truth of one's experience will emerge if only one can keep talking long enough in a whipped-up state of excitement. It takes more than this to make poetry. It just **does**.

Kaddish, by Allen Ginsberg, City Lights Books, 1961, $1.50.

19

THOM GUNN

As far as I am concerned, chiefest among all current suspects is Thom Gunn. He has already taken quite a beating from some very good American reviewers, notably John Thompson in the November, 1959 issue of *Poetry*. On the other hand, he is very highly regarded in England, wins all sorts of prizes there, and has things like this said about him by critics as acute, learned, and perceptive as Alfred Alvarez: "Gunn's *Fighting Terms* is the most impressive first book of poems since Robert Lowell's." I see him somewhat differently: as a fashionable, rote versifier of some skill and intelligence, the very perfect model of the young, Americanized British poet, writing solemnly about the sect of eagle-jacketed motorcycle riders and about Elvis Presley, who turns out (naturally!) to be a Symbol of impending war. All his work is smoothly executed. It can exercise your logical powers by putting before you a number of problems and resolving them neatly, but it has not the slightest power to touch you (or to touch me, perhaps I should say), or to make you feel that the situation with which it is dealing has any importance whatever, except as material for the kind of poems Gunn writes. Here are the motorcyclists:

> A minute holds them, who have come to go:
> The self-defined, astride the created will
> They burst away; the towns they travel through
> Are home for neither bird nor holiness,
> For birds and saints complete their purposes.
> At worst, one is in motion; and at best,
> Reaching no absolute, in which to rest,
> One is always nearer by not keeping still.

This sort of writing invites you to go on and on, line

after line, stanza after stanza, murmuring, " Yes, I think I see . . . Yes . . . Yes . . . Yes . . ." without actually assenting, or doing so only because the poet seems to have such utter confidence that what he is saying is true, and because some of the problems involved look pretty knotty, and would probably take some work to unravel. Eventually, though, you get a little tired of this diet of half-ideas, and begin to read the book all over again. And you ask questions like these, about the above quotation : Isn't it a little silly to characterize a group of sideburned toughs on Harley-Davidsons as " the self-defined, astride the created will " ? How about the reference to " the towns they travel through " ? Doesn't dragging in the supposed fact that birds and saints are *not* in the towns introduce a whole train of possibilities that, when examined, turns out to be completely irrelevant ? For example, what if birds and saints *were* in the towns ? Even though they " complete their purposes " (whatever that may mean), would this make any appreciable difference to the cyclists ? Is it even true that there are no birds in the towns ? I had thought previously that some birds can make a home anywhere. Perhaps I am being over-literal, but over-literalness comes to seem the only defense against Gunn's pedantic, pontifical manner, and his irritating pose as a universal Wise Man. From these poems you go back to the things and beings Gunn has written about, to the cities, the women, the magicians, the airedales of Yvor Winters, even to the motorcyclists, with relief, realizing that, after all, they're not, they *can't* be like these poems at all. And you feel, too, what a very sad thing it is that the poet in our time is an intellectual, and that his thinking sets him increasingly far from his subjects. If the poet's search is for " truth " and " reality," and for means by which to communicate these, one must drearily conclude that he is now farther from being able to do it than he has ever been. He has taken on a knowing, wise-seeming no-voice, a limbo voice like Gunn's, completely unconvincing, mannered, unmattering. He performs endless labours to make simple ideas complex and important-sounding. I have seldom read a duller book than *The Sense of Movement*, and I have nightmares thinking of the energy and the good intentions that went into it. Before the concrete of his approach and his " style " hardens around him, Gunn would do well to remember that his two favorite words, " will " and " define," are, in poetry, uneasy bed-fellows. It is not the will but the imagination that defines, or better still, holds, embodies, presents, and finally gives.

Gunn's book brings up the whole question of the recent influence of American on British poetry. In my opinion, it has not been good. The chief culprit, I am afraid, is Wallace Stevens, whose mannered artificiality and poetry-about-writing-poetry-about-poetry have driven large numbers of writers delightedly back into their shimmering, wordy sensibilities and buried them there. Gunn resembles Stevens no more than he does, say, Yvor Winters, but he has picked up the attitude that Stevens' work has fostered in the now influential next-to-youngest generation of American poets. According to this view, writing a poem is simply inventing a complex proposition about life or one of its manifestations, and illustrating it with whatever material appears to fit in. It seems to me that this leads to a particularly debilitated kind of puzzle-making sterility, where to over-complicate and then resolve is considered the criterion of artistic excellence. The great simplicities, the illuminations that should come like the sun from behind the cloud of ordinary perceptions and everyday judgments are not given a chance to come through, even if they could.

These moments are hard to have, hard to discover and embody. Why bother, when it is so easy to be a " career poet " and to make one's way in a society of opinion which gives good marks to poems like Gunn's ? Reading book after book of these poets, one is reminded of nothing so much as of Edmund Wilson's wonderful remark about the poems of Stephen Vincent Benêt, which are " just about the same kind of poetry that the ordinary man would produce if he'd gone in for writing poetry instead of for investment banking or selling real estate." No; we must look to writing in other languages than English for the creative *joie de vivre* that poetry must above all embody : to the poems of a thousand young Frenchmen full of sentimentalities at which Brooks and Warren might laugh, but which come out of an unself-consciousness that enables these writers to use their imagination at full stretch, resulting in poems that are as far as anything could possibly be from the constipated verses we are accustomed to reading, with their carefully market-tested and approved kind of significance. Or we would profit by going to the South Americans, especially to Neruda, whose magnificent abandon includes whole schools of wonderfully good and atrociously bad poets with the strength and delight of a demiurge. We have had enough of calculated effects in poetry, or at least of effects calculated as we have calculated them. Even the beatniks, though none has much imagination, can teach us things about opening up, for what we need most is the simple belief that a human being has said something because it matters.

The Sense of Movement, by Thom Gunn, University of Chicago Press, 1960, $2.75.

NED O'GORMAN

For a long time after I first read him, I didn't know what to make of Ned O'Gorman, and I am still not sure I do. In the beginning I felt I should admire what appeared to be his desperate lunges to get hold of something important, but having since gone back through *The Night of the Hammer* several times, grasping with only a shade less fervor than the poet himself, and continually coming up empty-handed, I no longer wish to pursue the assumption that the thing was ever there in the first place. Many of Mr. O'Gorman's titled pieces make intense, semi-articulate sounds and talk about God, but they do not seem to me to be poems, if organization and intelligence have anything to do with the definition of poetry. It is true enough that Mr. O'Gorman is not in the current mode of university-cultivated garden-poets, but in his case this fact doesn't seem to be in his favor. The structure of his work, when it is discernible at all, is so poor that most of his writings appear to be no more than arbitrary assemblages of half-observed people and objects, half-understood ideas and notions, thrown together in a slapdash, breathless, quasi-mystical and maddeningly assured manner, as if genius were at work, did we but have the sense to recognize it. I have never been brought so near to real agony by the remarks of a dust-jacket as I have by this one, with its talk of "delightful, sometimes wild gaiety," "gusty humor," and of Mr. O'Gorman's having "the poet's essential gift of making all things new." This last may very well be so, but if it is, one resolves, grimly and not without a certain amount of selfless dedication, to set about making them old again. The fact is that Mr. O'Gorman's work is absurdly farfetched, without being in the least imaginative. For example, who in his right mind, or in

24

his wrong mind, would want to begin a poem on Yeats with " He played too long on passion's calliope " ? Who could think there might be any conceivable kind of good, even comic good, in addressing his father in terms such as " O thou sweet dumb-bell " ? In addition to a great many other such failures of taste, Mr. O'Gorman must also own up to having written most of his book in prose : prose to make the prosiness of William Carlos Williams and Kenneth Rexroth sound like the singing of Elizabethan nightingales in comparison. Mr. O'Gorman's writing nearly all depends for its seeming energy on the primitive device of chopping up quite ordinary prose sentences, seeing to it that a fair number of the " lines " end in conjunctions or prepositions, and delivering the whole as verse :

> In the gamble for sacrifice Cain lost and
> Abel won; but winning in that family was a curse
> And Abel's head got broke apart for that.

What good moments there are in *The Night of the Hammer*—bees " with hammers in their wings " and a snake seen as " the twist of choking in the grass "—are hidden among such a deal of inconsequential, confident, earless chatter that one must hunt them down like protectively-colored animals. I suppose it may be construed as of some importance that they are there at all, but what we wish of a poet is poems, and there is none here, unless perhaps the title itself.

The Night of the Hammer, by Ned O'Gorman, Harcourt, Brace, 1958, $3.75.

25

ROBERT MEZEY

Robert Mezey is right in there with the rest of the poets of his generation, having studied " with John Crowe Ransom at Kenyon College and Paul Engle at the University of Iowa," and with this book has won the Lamont Poetry Prize, surely the most infallible badge of accepted-and-forgotten mediocrity our culture can bestow. Between the Yale Series of Younger Poets (if you feel in the mood for a sad, unbelieving laugh, look at Yale's list all the way back to the beginning, and *read* a few of the books) and the Lamont Prize, given to the likes of Ned O'Gorman and Donald Justice, I don't believe we could choose, and I'm glad we don't have to; both show the dismal state of our verse, and both go on awarding and publishing as though it mattered. This, of course, isn't Mr. Mezey's fault. And it isn't as though he can't write, either. He can; he writes very well, and he's not entirely school-gelded. The trouble is that the quality of his thought isn't much. His ideas are not interesting— at least not to me—and his commitment to experience is not deep and passionate enough, however much he may talk about passion and all its works, and is only connected to language at all because it is so easy, once you have learned, to connect " life " and words at a superficial level. I quote out of context because I haven't room for a whole poem, but one should be able to judge something of a poet's larger movements by his smaller ones :

> I am in love with you —
> And the moon, so lately spent,
> Will kiss your immaculate stillness
> In the dark pond of my consent.

Anyone could have fastened on such commonplaces and made them rhyme. But why should anyone want to? It is the *compulsion* to write one way rather than another, to say what one has to say in one way rather than another, the personal necessity for it, that makes good poets. And this Mezey seems to me to lack. He must struggle for the painful ground where his personality and the English language can inflict wounds on each other, and not lie down together like the lion and the lamb, not even suspicious at the beginning.

The Lovemaker, by Robert Mezey, The Cummington Press, 1961, (no price listed).

CHARLES OLSON

Charles Olson is one of the elder statesmen of the Grove Press poets, and his "Maximus" poems have been appearing in the very small and very rebellious magazines over the past several years. They have apparently gained a fairly enthusiastic reputation among the readers of these periodicals, and their collection has been anticipated with a good deal of excitement in some quarters, for at such a time the master plan was to be revealed, the relation of the parts to the whole shown; there was even speculation that the completed work would bring about a radically new kind of American poetry. Olson helped this supposition along by generously furnishing his followers with his theory of "projective" verse or "open" verse, which notion I should imagine he picked up from the French critic René Nelli, author of *Poésie Ouverte Poésie Fermée*. The kind of poetry which he describes is written, evidently, by means of a method entitled "composition by field." The poem, according to this, is "energy transferred from where the poet got it . . . to the reader." It must therefore be "a high energy-construct, and . . . an energy-discharge." Stripped of the language of physics, which in his use turns quickly to jargon, Olson's theory comes down to the simple and ancient one of organic form: "right form, in any given poem, is the only and exclusively possible extension of content under hand." As to the process by which this laudable goal may be reached, Olson tells us that "ONE PERCEPTION MUST IMMEDIATELY AND DIRECTLY LEAD TO A FURTHER PERCEPTION." These dicta, when taken in conjunction with a less easily understood set of ideas concerned with the relation of breathing to "the line," make up most of what Olson has to say about poetry. For the reference

28

of those who might wish to put it into action, I reproduce
Mr. Olson's key formula. " Put baldly," he says, " the
two halves are:
     the HEAD, by way of the EAR, to the SYLLABLE
     the HEART, by way of the BREATH, to the LINE."
If rightly applied to syllable and line, this process is
supposed to give " the play of the mind " which shows
" whether a mind is there at all."   In the poem—or the
" field," as Olson calls it—the syllables, lines, images,
sounds, and meanings " must be taken up as participants
in the kinetic of the poem just as solidly as we are
accustomed to take what we call the objects of reality."
These elements " are to be seen as creating the tensions
of the poem just as totally as those other objects create
what we know as the world."   Well, fine.   But this is
all nothing very new.   And when you come, finally, to
see that Olson's trump card, very nearly, is " the advantage of the typewriter," which ostensibly gives the
poet " for the first time " the " stave and the bar a
musician has had " it is pretty evident that Olson's
contribution to the aesthetics of poetry is likely to be
something less than epoch-making.   All the things he
says are in various ways true enough, but " projective
verse " has no claim on them; most of them are true of
any poetry, or at least of any that is worth reading.
Certainly organic form—the poem growing naturally from
its own materials and creating its own best internal re-
lations and overall shape—is the form that all good poems
must have: do have.   What Olson's notion of " open "
verse does is simply to provide creative irresponsibility
with the semblance of a rationale which may be defended
in heated and cloudy terms by its supposed practitioners.
All " schools " theorize endlessly, it may be noted.

The Maximus Poems themselves, issued in a handsome
format by Jonathan Williams' small and splendid Jargon/

Corinth Press, are reasonably interesting, though by no means as original as one might have been led to expect. I kept looking in them for the HEAD by way of the EAR to the SYLLABLE, but found only a great number of syllables which go back to Ezra Pound's head via the kind of jigsaw organizational techniques of William Carlos Williams' *Paterson*. Instead of " Mr. Paterson " we have Maximus, and instead of Paterson itself we have Gloucester, Mass. There is much of the history of Gloucester; there are lists of the crews of ships, what they carried, descriptions of their figureheads, and so on, evidently selected around one of Mr. Olson's principles, though I'm not sure which one. There are also a great many small, terse, prosy snapshots of Gloucester life both past and present, with Maximus now participating, now reading, now remembering, now dreaming. Some of these episodes are effective, especially a short prose section on cod-fishing, but I have difficulty in taking the whole seriously as a poem, as I do with *Paterson* also. Yet I have a weakness for long poems of this kind, for the *Cantos*, for *Paterson*, for *Maximus*, and particularly for the most obscure and ambitious of them all, David Jones' *The Anathémata*, which perhaps provides in its brilliant, thorny introduction the best justification for this kind of writing, for this kind of organization (or anti-organization), that could be made. Jones says, quoting Nennius (or whoever composed the introductory matter to the *Historia Brittonum*): coacervavi omne quod inveni: " I have made a heap of all that I could find." Jones then goes on to explain that he has allowed himself " to be directed by motifs gathered together from such sources as have by accident been available to me and to make a work of this mixed data." This, essentially, is what Olson has done also, and there is always some amount of fascination in seeing what things have been

made available to another's mind " by accident " and
have emerged in print as the details of a poem. In
presenting his material, Olson is both observant of the
way his world, including its history, looks and feels, and
determinedly bookish, with the cantankerous and
pedantic bluster of his self-educated colleagues Rexroth
and Edward Dahlberg. But with or without the help of
his theories, he has managed to write a few moderately
interesting sections of a long, unsuccessful poem which
must have been the labor of years, and these are worth
reading. The structure of the poem is only the structure
of fortuitous association plus the more obvious devices
and literary mannerisms of Pound and Williams, but his
mind seems to me quite a capable one, and at all points
is working hard to say what has been given it. That is
enough, because it has to be.

The Maximus Poems, by Charles Olson, Jargon-Corinth Book,
Citadel Press, 1960, $1.95.

HAROLD WITT

Harold Witt says that " close observation of what is most familiar—the regional and known—is the way to universals." This is probably true or at least it ought to be, but it is hard for me to believe that things like " the in absentia bees " constitute much of value in the way of " close observation." *The Death of Venus* displays a good deal of verbal busyness, an air of brilliant slap-dash improvisation, and very little real feeling or consequence. The poems only infrequently engage their subjects: instead, they take off from them, circle them, skirt them, and, in essence, play with them. Despite Witt's avowal of " close observation," his clever figures are maddeningly vague; to say of a " strayed opossum " that it is " disturbing as *stars* " (italics mine) is to say little more or less than that it is disturbing as diamonds, raspberries, head-colds, birds, airplanes, atomic bombs, or almost anything else you might want to pick, for all things, seen in some perspectives, are " disturbing " in some sense; in point of fact, stars are usually counted (unless you are Pascal) as relatively reassuring.

Most of his work shows Witt to be a decorative poet, the decorative being defined as the writer who, because he cannot say exactly the right thing, hopes to say the interesting thing. If, as Malcolm de Chazal maintains, poetry is the art of transmitting life, or the sense of life, at its most meaningful, then the presence of a living human being must somehow make itself felt behind the language. This does not happen in *The Death of Venus* any more than it does in the sardonic and contrived poems of Weldon Kees, which Witt's somewhat resemble. As must be apparent, I don't much like Witt's kind of writing. Nevertheless, he has an enviable store of energy, and obviously he loves the language. He may yet go through a thousand changes, and one of them may be the right one.

The Death of Venus, by Harold Witt, The Golden Quill Press, 1958, $2.50.

ANNE SEXTON

I—*To Bedlam And Part Way Back*

Anne Sexton's poems so obviously come out of deep, painful sections of the author's life that one's literary opinions scarcely seem to matter; one feels tempted to drop them furtively into the nearest ashcan, rather than be caught with them in the presence of so much naked suffering. The experiences she recounts are among the most harrowing that human beings can undergo: those of madness and near-madness, of the pathetic, well-meaning, necessarily tentative and perilous attempts at cure, and of the patient's slow coming back into the human associations and responsibilities which the old, previous self still demands. In addition to being an extremely painful subject, this is perhaps a major one for poetry, with a sickeningly frightening appropriateness to our time. But I am afraid that in my opinion the poems fail to do their subject the kind of justice which I should like to see done. Perhaps no poems could. Yet I am sure that Mrs. Sexton herself could come closer than she does here, did she not make entirely unnecessary concessions to the conventions of her literary generation and the one just before it. One can gather much of her tone and procedure from quotations like " You, Doctor Martin, walk/from breakfast to madness," and "All day we watched the gulls/striking the top of the sky/and riding the blown roller coaster." "Riding the blown roller coaster " is a kind of writing I dislike to such an extent that I feel, perhaps irrationally, that everyone else including Mrs. Sexton ought to dislike it, too, for its easy, A-student, superficially-exact " differentness " and its straining to make contrivance and artificiality appear natural.

One would hope that a writer of Mrs. Sexton's seriousness, and with her terrible story to tell, would avoid this
kind of thing at any price. Yet a large part of her book is
composed of such figures. In the end, one comes to the
conclusion that if there were some way to relieve these
poems of the obvious effort of trying to be poems, something very good would emerge. I think they would make
far better short stories, and probably in Mrs. Sexton's
hands, too, than they do poems. As they are, they lack
concentration, and above all the profound, individual linguistic suggestibility and accuracy that poems must have
to be good. As D. H. Lawrence once remarked in another
connection, they don't " say the real say." But Mrs. Sexton's candor, her courage, and her story are worth anyone's three dollars.

To Bedlam and Part Way Back, by Anne Sexton, Houghton Mifflin,
1960, $3.00.

II—*All My Pretty Ones*

In Anne Sexton's work the main sense is that of indignity—of being outraged by the world and its henchmen,
like surgeons and alcoholic lovers and dying parents. It
would be hard to find a writer who dwells more insistently
on the pathetic and disgusting aspects of bodily experience, as though this made the writing more real, and it
would also be difficult to find a more hopelessly mechanical approach to reporting these matters than the one she
employs.

Her attitude, widely cited as " compassionate," is
actually a curious compound of self-deprecatory
cynicism and sentimentality-congratulating-itself-on-not-
being-caught, as when Mrs. Sexton sees her stomach, after
surgery, as being "laced up like a football/for the game"
(as though footballs were laced up for games) or when she

says to " K. Owyne ": " I washed lobster and stale gin/off your shirt. We lived in sin/in too many rooms." Most of Mrs. Sexton's book is like this; her recourse to the studiedly off-hand diction favored by Randall Jarrell and Elizabeth Bishop and her habitual gravitation to the domestic and the " anti-poetic " seem to me as contrived and mannered as any romantic poet's harking after galleons and sunsets and forbidden pleasures.

The confessional quality in much recent verse, of which the works of Robert Lowell and W. D. Snodgrass are also cases in point, is giving rise to a new kind of orthodoxy as tedious as the garden-and-picture-gallery school of the forties and fifties. Though it is eminently orthodox in this respect, Mrs. Sexton's work seems to me very little more than a kind of terribly serious and determinedly outspoken soap-opera, and as such will undoubtedly have an appeal in some quarters.

All My Pretty Ones, by Anne Sexton, Houghton Mifflin, 1962, $3.00.

PHILIP BOOTH

When one writes of individual collections, one comes under the important obligation to submit as much as possible to each poet's viewpoint and his methods, and to understand the poems as " parts of a world " in a sense in which those of anthologies are not. I read Philip Booth's *Letter From a Distant Land* with this in mind, trying as best I could to see the poems as coming from and illuminating a crucial center. There is none, however. Booth's is an American Georgian poetry, thinly descriptive, replete with easy answers, vacant, amiably bucolic. There are many attempts to feel, or at least to talk about feelings, but precision is lacking, and therefore consequence. Booth tries hard to particularize, but, though he lists many objects, none comes through with the immediate and fierce *haecceitas* that good poems demand and exact. Instead of being concrete, as some reviewers have claimed, Booth's verse is actually quite diffuse and vague.

> We floated on hope at flood,
>   and over, over, the tide-
> sunk bar; there where the run
>   of current, the waving sun,
> showed clear on the waterglass
>   sand, on the seawind grass,
> how the islands were one.

Well, how *were* they one? Why is it " hope " on which the poet floats? Further, why " hope at flood," which implies some tremendous inner expectancy? True, Booth has previously stated that he and another had rowed ashore to swim " for love, a summer whim/When our limbs were all July," but that hardly seems adequate to justify the melting, grandiose assertion of the close. No; Booth's writing is undiscriminating in detail and thus mechanical, and so his feelings come to seem mechanical, too, and do not even seem possible without the full support of the Mode. Someone has remarked of this book that " there is not a really bad poem in it." This says exactly the reverse of what the statement intends. The fact that the poems are all no better than acceptably good, means, *sub specie aeternitatis*, that they are no better than unobtrusively or damnably bad; both good and bad, in these senses, will be equally lost. It reveals also, and devastatingly, one of the most pernicious results of the influence of the New Critics: the approval of poems on principle, as it were, if they sound like the thousands of others brought out by the same poetic weather. Booth sounds enough like the other poets his age and of his time to be all of them in one; in addition, he has a strain of complacent sentimentality which I find very much not to my liking. It may be that he will turn out well; I hope so. As far as I am concerned, however, his beginning does not indicate this as a strong possibility.

Letter From a Distant Land, by Philip Booth, Viking, 1957, $3.00.

IN THE PRESENCE OF ANTHOLOGIES

NEW POETS OF ENGLAND AND AMERICA I (1957)

In a sense, every poem of every new book is presided over and judged by an imminent Anthology. Anthologies are perhaps the most important harbingers of lastingness that a writer's work may know during his lifetime; thus they have come to seem a kind of trial immortality for all good poems. In them, poets look for their names and their best or most typical poems, or their atypical, one-shot successes with fear, pride, satisfaction, and awe: in the presence of anthologies the mighty tremble; the lesser know fantastic hope, and the plainly unworthy are exalted. Doubts are many, on the part of the anthologist no less than on that of the poets, for what type of book is more open to attack? Anyone who reviews or even reads it is almost certain to use it merely to throw out in favour of the one *he* would edit, if he could ever get round to it, or if he were ever asked. Into the presence of this celestial and awesome Book all others come at their own risk, and are withered in the impossible light of Heaven. Reading earthly collections does, however, lead one to certain conclusions about the function of the genre, which is not at all what we sometimes suppose it to be. The *raison d'être* of the anthology is only secondarily to indicate trends, groups, schools, and periods, or to show what the young are writing, or what the old have written at different times, under different cultural conditions, or to demonstrate what Louis Untermeyer considers to be *A Treasury of Great Poems*. It is not to present a reflection of " the sensibility of an era " as seen in the eyes of its editors, or, more fragmentarily, in those of its poets. It is to lead readers to the poets on their home ground, their own books, where they present their worlds as fully and deeply as they are able. Such, especially, is the value of a book like *The New*

Poets of England and America (I), since only a few of these writers are at all well-known. Reading through *New Poets*, I found myself, after a first, free-wheeling and very enjoyable game of " Put-in, Take-out," objecting less and less to the selections, for the book is superbly edited, and, though its inclusions and exclusions are questionable in many cases, most of these poets have every right to admission, being as well as any others representative of a generation that has as yet exhibited very little passion, urgency, or imagination. I am still disturbed at not seeing John Logan, Wilfred Watson, Claire McAllister, and Ernest Sandeen, from this side of the Atlantic. From among the English poets, I miss Burns Singer, Christopher Logue, the brilliant Hilary Corke, and, most of all, Robert Conquest, editor of the important *New Lines* collection, and certainly superior to seven-tenths of these writers. The editors promise subsequent editions, however, and it may be that one day we shall have them all, and shall then be able to construct our ideal Anthology merely by exclusion.

Aside from Robert Lowell, represented only by his first and best work, *New Poets* shows only a few American writers who could not be exchanged one for the other without appreciable loss. Two of the editors, Hall and Simpson, are good; Hall is tasteful and delicate, with a generous sense of humor and a nice understanding of structural balance; Simpson is agreeable and sharp, using history lightly and imaginatively in "The Green Shepherd," and building an enveloping and moving dreamwork in " I Dreamed That in a City Dark as Paris." I also liked poems by Howard Nemerov, William Jay Smith, Howard Moss, William Meredith, and Reed Whittemore. The rest all seem to be each other.

The fault of most of this poetry—and perhaps of most poetry—is that one simply doesn't believe it. One longs in vain for some standard by which to measure the capacity of works of art to reach us " where we live " : to be able to say something definitive about the mysterious enlightening conjunction between the good poem and the inner life of the beholder, without which poetry is an exercise differing from any other linguistic usage only in format. It is easy enough to like the poems in *New Poets*; they fulfill many of our notions of what poems should be; they are by turns clever (Amis), elegant (Hecht and Wilbur), ploddingly " sincere " (Wright), learned (Davie and Gunn), humbly aspiring (Pack and Justice), funny (Causley and Whittemore), ingenious (Coulette), and sardonic (Finkel), but never any of these things in a way that matters very much. It is easy to like them, but difficult to care about them. Most of these are occasional poets; most have been schooled or have learned to pick up pretty nearly any scene or object from memory and make acceptable poetic currency of it. Yet this wider field of choice actually reduces the chances for an absolute and personal fatality of viewpoint to occur: the Inevitable tends to get blurred, obscured, and finally swallowed up by the imploring crowd of pretty and quite serviceable Possibles. Facility is not alone at fault; we have given a charming and deliberate smallness far more than its due. There are many poets here who may eventually emerge as significant, but at present, as this excellent selection makes clear, most of them are exemplars of the thing they must overthrow in order to do so.

The main English bloc here is formed of the so-called " Movement " poets, and the American, less well-defined but still quite identifiable, of the university-taught, New-Criticism-oriented writers whom I am tempted to label collectively the " School of Charm." Though assuredly not of great moment, the " Movement " poets are considerably more interesting than ours. In their work, an uneasy alliance has been joined between Auden and Empson, and fitted with a special Outlook best exemplified in the poems of John Wain (not represented here) and Kingsley Amis. There are the familiar " lists " from Auden (" The . . . the . . .the . . . /The . . . the . . . the . . the . . ") and many waggish instances of zeugma (" . . tickled up with ghosts/That brandish warnings or an abstract noun "). There are the terse, laconic statements learned from Empson (" For one month afterwards the eye stays true . . ."). But these devices are only background for the Outlook, which may be defined as a mutually-understood helplessness, in the face of which, much as Hemingway's hero displays " grace," the poet must show wit. I am reminded by the Outlook of nothing so much as of T. E. Hulme's statement that " philosophical syntheses and ethical systems are possible only in arm-chair movements. They are seen to be meaningless as soon as we get into a bus with a dirty baby and a crowd." Amis, particularly, is so strongly in sympathy with the man happy to forget his " philosophical syntheses " under such circumstances that he appears continually to be half-apologizing for writing at all. Reading Amis' own book, *A Case of Samples,* one sees that his real theme is this embarrassment about writing : his assumption, which he expects us to share, that it is amusingly futile at best: he not only believes, but must *confess* he believes his poems bear not the slightest real relation to the tiresome, routine, scrubby existences that people live. Yet Amis is not empty; only thin, bright, and somewhat brittle. He is amusing, and should make his contribution to light verse, wherein he is perfectly assured, quite funny, and certainly in fashion.

Of the other " Movement " writers included in *New Poets*, only Philip Larkin is worth considering. He is said to exemplify the best of the group's work, and I am inclined to agree with the judgment. He is assuredly a great deal more interesting than Thom Gunn, John Holloway, or Donald Davie, all of whom seem to me derivative, cautious, and nearly profitless. Unlike these, Larkin is in a continuously right and meaningful relation to his material. Without straining in the least, he gets a little more out of each subject than one would have thought likely; one understands at last that this small, characteristic difference between his poems and the quite ordinary ones he might have written stems simply from his warm, penetrating way of seeing his subjects, and of thinking clearly about them. He has an easy, conversational voice that strikes me as being very nearly flawless in pitch, and a tender gravity I find most attractive.

In keeping with my earlier pronouncement about the " true function " of anthologies, I want to mention two young English writers whom I had not previously known, in hopes that the reader will be led to seek out their other publications, as I intend to do. Geoffrey Hill and Jon Silkin are both under thirty, and promise much. Hill's " Genesis " is one of the few very fine poems in *New Poets*. I can think of no better compliment to pay Hill than to say I was all but persuaded that, were God a very talented young poet, the six days of the Creation might very well have been as the poem says they were.

Silkin is a strange, breathless, visionary yet energetic poet who deals with the world largely in terms of the deaths of birds, insects, and animals, viewing these not only as portents of human death and perhaps of universal dissolution, but as happenings in themselves unfathomable: terrible, unforgivable. His work brings home to us again the fact that the poet must, inevitably, be obsessed: that it is his obsession that gives urgency and point to his use of the craft, being the thing that the words must at all costs embody. Beside Silkin's pathetic and passionate writing one is eager to forget the *New Poets*' pages and pages of neatly worked-up situations, such as " Or let me think I pause beside a door/And see you in a bodice of Vermeer . . . " and the countless other wearisome rehearsals of known, usable qualities that seem mostly the property of the American contingent, here.

The New Poets of England and America, edited by Donald Hall, Robert Pack, and Louis Simpson, Meridian Books, 1957, $1.45.

There are four or five main ways of reacting to poems, and they all matter. In ascending order of importance they are (a) " This probably isn't so, and even if it w e r e I couldn't care less," (b) " This may be true enough as far as it goes, but, well . . . so what?" (c) " This is true, or at least convincing, and therefore I respond to it differently than I do to poems in the first two categories," and (d) " This is true with a kind of truth at which I could never have arrived by myself, but its truth is better than the one I had believed." The first two classifications are useful because they are what we feel about bad poems, very bad ones in (a) and half-bad or unsuccessfully realized ones in (b). In (c) are most of the poems we like well enough to call " good " in reviews and to which we may want to return occasionally, and in (d) are those we continue to call great when conversing only with ourselves, and which we would hope to die hearing or remembering. Almost all writers of verse aspire simply to reside in (c), and many a solid reputation—such as that of Robert Graves—has been founded on just such a semi-permanent residence, which is by no means as easy of attainment as I may make it seem. Even those whom we call " major " poets catch only a few glimpses of the world I have designated (d), or at most stand for a handful of moments in that bewildering light, in the certainty that they are bringing about an entirely new kind of human communication compounded of about equal parts of the commonality of all mankind and the unique particularity of the poet's vision and his language. The achievement of even a small but steadily authentic flame is immensely difficult, as we all know, and requires, as well as a great deal of luck, a lifelong attention to those means by which we might best hope to feed it. With each poem, the difficulties come at us from all sides anew. How far, the poet thinks, should I entrust my poem to the flux of images and memories that are its only hope? The stream of consciousness (and unconsciousness) is the source of all good things, but it is also the source of all bad things. If I inhibit it with too many rules, it is likely to give me nothing, and I will end up writing a poetry of the pure will, like Lee Anderson's (true, Paul Valéry insisted that he wrote this kind, but if so his will was a better imagination than my imagination). The opposite thing to do is to let everything out, and for a brief dazzling moment which some poets never outlive, this looks like the answer, the philosopher's stone, the Comstock Lode of poetry. Abandoned to that stream, and with all kinds of subterranean creatures thrusting words into your mouth by the bucketful, it is hard not to ride thus forever, singing and shouting whatever comes to mind. If someone were to tell you that your " song " was only a kind of monstrousness that has to be understood and ordered according to some principle to be meaningful, you might be likely to bring up in refutation what the French refer to as the Surrealist Breakthrough, and the marvelous poems of Éluard and Desnos, which (these poets assure us at great length) could not have come forth in any other way. And if you are young, and if you get the proper kind of encouragement from your elders, men like Kenneth Rexroth and Charles Olson, you can coast down-stream forever, perfectly mindless and jubilant. This is, I think, a fair description of the writers in Mr. Donald Allen's anthology. And to an era weary of over-refined, university-pale subtleties they look interesting; at least they look *different*. Nothing on God's earth can shut them up, and the fact that a good many of their own kind and a few curio-seekers from other walks of life listen to them bellow in coffee-houses convinces those who wish to be convinced that they are "bringing poetry back to the public," restoring it to its true role, making it prophetic, and so on. Meanwhile their mentors keep telling the genteel, mildly-interested middle-brow public that this is a "real movement": that, as Mr. Rexroth said recently in the *New York Times* Book Review section, these writers are aware of their "unchanging responsibility to poetry's most ancient utterances," that this one is "unquestionably the best" of the lot and that that one is a "rough, startlingly honest poet," and so on, as if these estimates were indeed of some value, much as if I were to say that a grade-school sprinter displays "startling leg drive" or is "explosive off the blocks" and said nothing at all of what would happen to him if he were to line up on the same track with Dave Sime or Armin Hary. The fact is that few of those who fill up the 454 pages of *The New American Poetry* can write a lick. These few are occasionally good in some of the ways in which it matters to be good, but put against a really intelligent and resourceful poet like Howard Nemerov even they show up pretty drably. The fact that a reasonably large segment of the reading public might now be persuaded that the "New Poets" are "real" and that poets like Nemerov are only "mandarin" writers (as Rexroth, using Cyril Connolly's term, says) indicates as nothing else has done for a long time how little we really care about poetry, how little we love it for what it is to us (and not for what we have been told it is), and above all how little we have learned about it.

Perhaps poetry is by nature a realm where only extremes and things of more than life size, more than life intensity are valid. But there is a vast difference between the extremes of Rimbaud, a genius who screamed, and Allen Ginsberg, an ordinary and somewhat pretentious man who screams. It may be, too, that the answer deserved by the sober constipation of the Yvor Winters school and the chatty, knowledgeable aesthetic elegance of the likes of Anthony Hecht and George Starbuck is the aggressive gabble of the "Beats" and the other and similar poets whom Mr. Allen puts before us. And perhaps, again, what we really want (or perhaps I had better say what *I* really want) has very little to do with either.

When I stop to examine them, as I frequently do these days, I find that my tastes in poetry are actually quite simple. I wish merely to be able to feel and see and respond to whàt the poet is saying, and with as much strength and depth as possible. The difficulty is that much contemporary (and other) poetry is made up of a number of totally unconvincing postures, and induces a kind of disbelief in the reader completely different from that cited by Coleridge. It is a disbelief which refuses to be suspended either willingly or unwillingly, for it is occasioned by a growing certainty that the writer has wilfully betrayed his own experience. The most unconvincing of these postures—all so remarkably alike that they posit a new poetic conformity-in-anarchy which may well presage the death of all authentic expression in this generation—are to be found in Mr. Allen's collection. If the first blow is dealt the reader's belief in the poem by any hint of insincerity, this belief is simply annihilated by such yowling for attention (not in order to communicate anything, but merely to be noticed, to be discovered saying something ostensibly poetic and/or philosophical) as this "line" from Michael McClure: OH BEAUTY BEAUTY BEAUTY BEAUTY BEAUTY BEAUTY IS HIDEOUS. I think this is not an unfair sample of Mr. McClure's approach, if such it may be called. Mr. Ginsberg's is similar, though even less interesting, despite the fact that some of it has to do with narcotics and homosexuality. Ginsberg's comic abilities,

49

which I still enjoy, are not much in evidence here, which is a shame. But then Mr. Ginsberg's poems are not the best in this anthology, either, though certainly the most publicized, and so my regret over the omission of his poem about the luggage room at the Greyhound bus station is balanced by some work by other writers in which there are certain glimmers of talent which may eventually lead to better poetry than these poets are able to come up with at present. Of these, Gary Snyder comes closest to valid expression. The example of Pound has helped him, and that probably explains his superiority to the others. I think, too, that Robert Duncan is quite imaginative, though somewhat pretentious, and that there are some good passages in the selections from Charles Olson, Paul Blackburn, Paul Carroll, Larry Eigner, Jonathan Williams, and Denise Levertov. The rest, as far as I am concerned, are a complete and dead loss, and must bore even their authors.

Both the public and "critical" (or Rexrothian) success and the actual failure of these people (or the majority of them, at any rate) can be traced to the absence in each of them of what W. H. Auden calls "the censor": the faculty or indwelling being which determines what shall and what shall not come into a poem, and which has the final say as to how the admitted material shall be used. It is basically the same as Coleridge's "architectonic" faculty: that which builds the good details into coherent wholes. But if everything we come out with is called "good," what basis is there for the selection of the real good? Much less the ordering of authentic materials into significant communicative structures? If I feel a little guilty about using this kind of academic language I do so with some defiance, for I recognize that even academism, much as I have inveighed against it in the past, is (as Dr. Winters tells us) a defense of the mind, and so of the only way in which permanently valuable poetry may be written. It is quite true—and has been amply demonstrated over the last twenty years—that the censor can censor you to death, and can cut off the life-stream of the unconscious entirely, or poison it in subtle and sterilizing ways. To make matters even more complicated, the censor can even write poems out of virtually nothing, much as if a man were to build a house only of nails, or as if a poem were to fancy itself the subject of Roy Campbell's justly celebrated quatrain about the South African novelists, using " the snaffle and the curb " on a non-existent horse. And this is not good, either. But when the stream of images is rich and full and the censor is at his best: when he (or it) knows what to look for and seize on and what to do with it when it appears, poetry has its only legitimate chance to come into being. It is precisely this chance that the " Beats " are systematically denying themselves, with the help of (again) Mr. Rexroth, William Carlos Williams, Charles Olson, and editors like Donald Allen, who has the temerity to label his book *The New American Poetry*. What he has given us, instead, is an enormous amount of fairly low-grade whale-fat, at least part of which might, with the help of the censor, render down into usable oil. But this is something we are unlikely ever to see happen. There is too much encouragement given it to remain what it is: " natural."

The New American Poetry: 1945-60, edited by Donald A. Allen, Grove Press, 1960, $1.95.

THE SECOND BIRTH

THE SECOND BIRTH

Most people interested in poetry (which means those who write it, those who aspire to write it, and those who criticize it) must notice at one time or another how few " born poets " there are, and how many poets : how few, like Orpheus and Rimbaud and Dylan Thomas, who find themselves early in life with the complete instrument in their hands, and have only to accord its strings to make the rocks dance and posterity rejoice: how few of these there are, and how many of the other kind. These last must all hope for the Second Birth, brought on slowly if at all by years of the hardest kind of work, much luck, much self-doubt, many false starts, and the difficult and ultimately moral habit of trying each poem, each line, each word, against the shifting but finally constant standards of inner necessity. As the words come to him, the poet must be eternally and ruthlessly vigilant against claiming what is not really his: against fastening on a good Audenesque or Empsonian line, say, and using it because it occurred to him instead of to Auden or Empson. Through enough such renunciations, he may, if he is fortunate and has the will and the time, come to define and thence to explore his own uniquely human segment of the common consciousness, and if in so doing he develops a characteristic style suited to express his discoveries, he will have succeeded at least to some degree in the essential task of the poet of the Second Birth; he will have obliterated or reduced to unimportance the standing distinction between the "born" and the "made" poet. The poet of the Second Birth must strive all his life to become, in Pierre-Jean Jouve's luminous phrase, " master of a superior secret." The secret does not, of course, reside in a complete originality, which does not and could not exist. It dwells, rather, in the development of personality, with its unique weight of experience and memory, as a writing instrument, and in the ability to give literary influence a new dimension which has the quality of this personality as informing principle. The Second Birth is largely a matter of self-criticism and endless experiment, presided over by an unwavering effort to ascertain what is most satisfying to the poet's self as it develops, or as it remains more clearly what it has always been. That the Second Birth can be attained in our time as in any other, we have as examples W. S. Graham, who rose from perfectly terrible imitations of Thomas to a strong, confident style utilizing elements of Scottish balladry, but based, largely, also, on snatches of conversation overheard in pubs, on street-corners, and in the shipyards of the River Clyde. There is Theodore Roethke, who began as a poet so traditional that even Yvor Winters approved of him, and then, beginning again, ranged through the strange hot-house world of inspired baby-talk and "pre-poetry" of *The Lost Son* back to a formal verse that really counts. Perhaps the most striking case in point is the marvellous John Berryman, who began quite ordinarily as one of the better disciples of Yeats and Auden, and after twenty years of wrestling with the problems of syntax as it operates within the poetic line, emerged to create, in the birth sequence of *Homage To Mistress Bradstreet*, what is to my mind the most daring and successful rendering of human experience ever to appear in American poetry. If we hold the example of these poets enough in mind, the while honouring them for the difficult and valuable thing they have done: if we realize it is not enough simply to write "the best poems of which we are capable," for these are more than apt to sound like (or even to *be*) the second or third-best poems of Empson or Auden or Thomas or someone else: if we hold out, line by line, as if forever, for the poems that are as near as we can get them to being our own, we shall have some chance of saving our age from the fate of inconsequence, adequateness, and imitation that is threatening to render it impotent. The belief in the value of one's personality has all but disappeared from our verse. Yet the inexhaustible vitality and importance of writing are there, and nowhere else. Berryman and Roethke show us this, and so do Robert Penn Warren, Lawrence Durrell, Edwin Muir, and Richard Eberhart. Let the poets of my generation ask as much of themselves.

THEODORE ROETHKE

Theodore Roethke seems to me the finest poet now writing in English. I reiterate this with a certain fierceness, knowing that I have to put him up against Eliot, Pound, Graves, and a good many others of deservedly high rank. I do it also cheerfully, however, for stating his own idiosyncratic and perhaps indefensible views is part of a reviewer's business. I think Roethke is the finest not so much because of his beautifully personal sense of form but because of the way he sees and feels the aspects of life which are compelling to him. The powerful, almost somnambulistic statements of his observations and accountings come to us as from the bottom of the " deep well of unconscious cerebration " itself, or from a Delphic trance where everything one says is the right, undreamed-of, and known-by-the-gods-all-the-time thing that should be and never is said. The best of Roethke's poems are very nearly as frightening and necessary as " darkness was upon the face of the deep," and as simple and awesome as " let there be light." It is this world of perpetual genesis, his own genesis, recurring, continually available if only the perceiver is up to it in mind and body, that Roethke has somehow got down in words. The few objects that define his personality—stones, flowers, sunlight, wind, woman, darkness, animals, fish, insects, birds—tell his entire story, and the changes and similarities he finds among them are his poems. They are simple, tragic, profound, and unutterably joyful. They are, and will be, permanent parts of our perception of reality, and one feels guilty of an unjust act, of a dislocation of nature, in referring to them as " literature " at all.

Words for the Wind, by Theodore Roethke, Indiana University Press, 1961, $1.75.

KENNETH PATCHEN

Often at night, when I see that, indeed, the sky is a " deep throw of stars," I think of a poet named Kenneth Patchen, who once told me that it is. Because of this and a few other passages I remember years after first reading them, I have tried to keep track of Patchen, and have gone through most of his books (all, in fact, except *Sleepers Awake*, which I abandoned in despair). I have heard recently that he has joined the " San Francisco School," but in reality he was its only permanent member twenty years before the group was ever conceived in the impatient mind of Kenneth Rexroth, and is still, despite having produced a genuinely impassable mountain of tiresome, obvious, self-important, sprawling, sentimental, witless, preachy, tasteless, useless poems and books, the best poet that American literary expressionism can show. Occasionally, in fragments and odds and ends nobody wants to seek out any more, he is a writer of superb daring and invention, the author of a few passages which are, so far as I can tell, comparable to the most intuitively beautiful writing ever done. He is a poet not so much in form as in essence, a condition of which we should all be envious, and with which we should never be satisfied. To evoke the usual standards of formal art in Patchen's case is worse than meaningless. He cannot give anything through the traditional forms (those who suggest that he ought at least to try should take a look at some of the rhymed poems in *Before the Brave*). I do not like to read most of Patchen's work, for it seems to me a cruel waste, but he somehow manages to make continuing claims on my attention that other more consistent poets do not. If there is such a thing as pure or crude imagination, Patchen has it, or has had it. With it he has made twenty-five years of Notes, in the form of scrappy, unsatisfactory, fragmentarily brilliant poems, for a single, unwritten cosmic Work, which bears, at least in some of its parts, analogies to the prophetic books of Blake. Yet the words, the phrases, and the lines that are supposed to make up the individual pieces almost never coalesce, themselves, into wholes, because Patchen looks upon language as patently unworthy of the Vision, and treats it with corresponding indifference and contempt. This is the reason he is not a good writer, or a good prophet, either: this, and the fact that his alternately raging and super-sentimental view of things is too violent, centerless, convulsive, and one-dimensional to be entirely convincing. But he has made and peopled a place that would never have had existence without him: the realm of the " Dark Kingdom," where " all who have opposed in secret, are . . . provided with green crowns," and where the vague, powerful figures of fantasmagoric limbo, the dream people, and, above all, the mythic animals that only he sees, are sometimes as inconsolably troubling as the hallucinations of the madman or the alcoholic, and are occasionally, as if by accident, rendered in language that accords them the only kind of value possible to this kind of writing: makes them obsessive, unpardonable, and magnificent. It is wrong of us to wish that Patchen would " pull himself together." He has never been together. He cannot write poems, as the present book heartlessly demonstrates. But his authentic and terrible hallucinations infrequently come to great good among the words which they must use. We should leave it at that, and take what we can from him.

When We Were Here Together, by Kenneth Patchen, New Directions, 1957, $3.50.

HOWARD NEMEROV

I—*The Salt Garden*

Howard Nemerov is a fine poet in the process, here, of
becoming a finer one. His is a tough-minded, learned,
subtle, and ironic lyricism, determined at all times not
to let the world bring in anything poetic form can't
handle. There is not a really bad poem in his book.
What you do miss, though, is a sense of the poems
speaking themselves out, or ever thinking that they ought
to speak themselves out, beyond the poet's assured and
confident and somewhat predictable idiom into their own
uniqueness and necessity. In these tight, nervously off-
hand stanzas, the means are too obviously well-satisfied
at being " adequate "; there is not enough evidence of the
exploratory, the big-thing-just-missed, or got-hold-of-in-
part, that we feel we can legitimately expect of a talent
as promising as his.

You are inclined to think of Nemerov as a " resourceful " poet, and he is, very. The resources are those you
might imagine: Auden, Eliot, and, more pronouncedly,
Yeats, but more especially yet, those of a kind of climate
of " modern poetry " that these earlier figures have dis-
tilled. This weather of custom makes it possible for one
to pick his structures and even his attitudes from the air,
and it is doubly nice, considering the ease with which
this may be done, to be told that one is " in the
tradition ": that one is " consolidating " (or even " im-
proving ") what one's predecessors have but indicated.
But the " tradition," considered in this sense, makes a
very real danger of " adequacy," or idiomatic accept-
ability: makes it, in fact, a species of shallow and ex-
pectant death-bed of originality, of the personal and
individuating reaction to things which in large part

determines the value of the poet's work. I don't mean to offer Nemerov as a sacrifice to this (perhaps dubious) conjectural machinery, for he is too gifted a poet to be a perfect or even a particularly good example of the tendency I describe. Nevertheless, it seems to me that he would do well to watch himself closely, or abandon himself less shrewdly, perhaps, for the next few years, when he writes.

Nemerov is a very easy poet to read; you like him immediately. He always gives you " something to think about," even in the lighter poems, the *New Yorker*ish ones, and you are inclined to waive the feeling that you have thought about it before, with more vital connections between you and the world, in the work of Yeats and Auden. Despite the uneasy suspicion that many of the poems are better exercises than poems, you do feel, when you have finished the book, that Nemerov is beginning to limit and perfect his own thing, or two things, rather: the satiric song with learned overtones, the resigned, knowing, intellectual lyric, and, on the other hand, the casual-serious meditation from nature, in which the schooled modern intelligence looks through or past its burden of knowledge into the brute Fact of an aspect of the surrounding world.

> . . . these trees were here, are here,
> Before King Hannibal had elephants
> Or Frederick grew his red beard through the table
> Or Mordecai hung Haman at the gate.
> The other Ahasuerus has not spat
> Nor walked nor cobbled any shoe, nor Joseph
> So much as dreamed that he will found the Corn
> Exchange Bank in the baked country of Egypt.
> Not even those burnt beauties are hawked out,
> By the angry Beginner, on Chaos floor

Where they built Pandemonium the Palace
Back in the high old times.   Most probably
Nothing will happen.   Even the Fall of Man
Is waiting, here, for someone to grow apples;
And the snake, speckled as sunlight on the rock
In the deep woods, still sleeps with a whole head
And has not begun to grow a manly smile.

The poetry of the present age in America, the forties
and fifties, has its exemplar in Nemerov, I think.   He is
in my opinion the best poet under forty-five that we have,
with the possible exception of Richard Wilbur.   I should
like to see him break out a little, though, write a few bad
poems, even, and then come at the thing another way,
through more " Deep Woods " and " Sanctuaries," keeping one hand on what he has won in the " Dialectical
Songs."   It may be that the long sequence " The Scales
of the Eyes " is the poem I am wishing for him.   Certainly
it contains many impressive things.   It is concerned with
spiritual definition: with the Why of belonging " here,"
at this place and time rather than another.   Nemerov's
" here " is between the city and the sea, between process
and permanence, between the fact and the symbol.   The
interplay of figures, the star and the pool, the vine, the
bloodvessel, the snowfall, the waiting animal, the spider's
web, the bird, seems at first a little discursive, but each
of these entities comes to hold, through quiet, skillful
shading, a powerful and unique particularity.

The low sky was mute and white
And the sun a white hole in the sky
That morning when it came on to snow;
The hushed flakes fell all day.

63

The hills were hidden in a white air
And every bearing went away,
Landmarks being but white and white
For anyone going anywhere.

All lines were lost, a noon bell
I heard sunk in a sullen pool
Miles off. And yet this patient snow,
When later I walked out in it,

Had lodged itself in tips of grass
And made its mantle bridging so
It lay upon the air and not the earth
So light it hardly bent a blade.

Yet, despite its impressiveness, the poem misses a total, felt unity (though I should not be prepared to argue this with Mr. Kenneth Burke, whose reading of the poem draws on sources of interpretation to which I can pretend no knowledge at all). The individual poems seem to me to achieve more by themselves than the sequence does; the poem is somehow split and portioned out among its symbols and approaches instead of being concentrated, drawn in upon them.

I hope I am not ungrateful to Nemerov in this summary. He is a poet who rouses your fears that he will spend a great deal of time sewing himself a uniform which fits part of him perfectly, provided he exorcises the Fire-Bringer, who is harder to measure. I should like to see Nemerov a Power Among Us, not written off as a " careful minor artisan." The good poems here, " The Sanctuary," most of " The Scales of the Eyes," " Deep Woods," " The Priest's Curse on Dancing," (though when will someone point out that in the much-praised " I Only Am Escaped Alone to Tell Thee," the plaintive " But all that whalebone came from whales " is not really adequate, structurally, to bind the two parts of the central metaphor?) make this by far the poet's best book. It is better, I assume, to say a few hard things of it, hoping they will help the poet even if he sends them off to Hell, than cheerful half-truths, " the nice things one could say " if one looked the book over with an eye toward determining what they might be.

The Salt Garden, by Howard Nemerov, Atlantic-Little, Brown, 1955, $3.00.

II—*Selected Poems*

I am of Howard Nemerov's generation, in age about midway between him and W. S. Merwin. I have never had great hopes for the poets of my time, since it has seemed for years that the writers who came to maturity just before, during, and immediately after the second war were to survive only as human beings, settling into the genteel, face-saving poverty and sterility of academic life and having their poems published simply because they were the only poets there were, and that they (or we) were never to count as poets at all, except as a kind of Georgian era that would be annihilated by some new revolution of the word, much as Pound and Eliot blew the literary world apart around 1912. After reading Mr. Nemerov's *New and Selected Poems,* however, and after noting that James Wright, Jon Silkin, Geoffrey Hill and W. S. Graham are of the same generation: after noting, too, that those poets whose early work I most deplored for its neatness, correctness, and deadness— poets like Merwin and James Merrill—have not died as artists but developed toward other and better modes of

65

expression: after reading the work of the "Beat" poets of the ilk of Ginsberg, Corso, and Ferlinghetti (surely the most ludicrously bad of them all) and the defenses of same by the older Beats like Rexroth, none of whom is fit to appear on the same page (or platform) with Nemerov, Silkin, or any of the others I have mentioned: after all these things I begin to see my generation somewhat differently than before, and am a great deal more encouraged over its possibilities than I have ever been. That a new poetry of some kind is coming I have no doubt. But it will not be the anarchic collectivism of the Beats, nor will it be based on the sentimental eroticism of Rexroth or the bookish pastiche of Olson. It will not be the airless aestheticism of the forties, either. I cannot of course make any sure prediction as to what its outlines might be like, but if it is to prove of any value at all it will have to find a way to use the intelligence at full stretch, and to turn it into an instrument of liberation rather than constriction: a means by which the intellect can function without inhibiting whatever personal vision and imagination the writer may possess. The operation of such an essentially poetic intelligence can be seen in the newest work of Howard Nemerov, and in great and heartening abundance. Nemerov is one of the few poets I have ever encountered who can turn the sometimes rather grim business of reading through the poems of a book into a profoundly enjoyable experience without sacrificing a jot of intensity. He is one of the wittiest and funniest poets we have, and there are whole sections of his book which might easily be passed over as clever light verse by clever, light readers. And it is true, too, that in his most serious poems there is an element of mocking, or self-mocking. But the enveloping emotion that arises from his writing is helplessness: the helplessness we all feel in the face of the events of our time, and of life itself: the helplessness one feels as one's legitimate but chronically unfair portion in all the things that can't be assuaged or explained. And beneath even this feeling is a sort of hopelessly involved acceptance and resignation which has in it far more of the truly tragic than most poetry which deliberately sets out in quest of tragedy. I won't go on and on, and I won't name what I think are Mr. Nemerov's best poems, for I want each reader to find them for himself, and for all opinions to differ and for each beholder to defend his own view, if necessary, with his life. But I do wish to end by saying that Nemerov has earned the best that his poetic intelligence, his imaginative censor, can do for him, and that this censor, far from limiting him by putting up barbed wire at his boundaries, is busy showing him every day just how those boundaries may be pushed back, little by little, so that what stands inside them is earned ground, and will remain his. For what we all want, in the end, is just such a censor: a poetry-knowledgeable and poetry-divining being who could only be ours, and who is a good deal more alive and kicking than we are, is more vitally conscious and certainly more poetically responsible than we, more able to tell the good from the bad, the essential from the inessential, the borrowed from the new. He is, really, all we have: the best of ourselves as writers. The value of the censor, the notion of the censor, lies not with Mr. Auden, who defined him and cleverly gave him a name which I have been using uncleverly: the value is not in the name but in the thing, the demonstration of its timeless importance and purpose: the poems of good poets.

Selected Poems, by Howard Nemerov, University of Chicago Press, 1960, $3.50.

HAYDEN CARRUTH

I—The Crow and The Heart

Hayden Carruth has been around a long time, as "younger poets" go. Up to now, I have never been favorably impressed with anything of his I have seen, and have passed him off as one among many of the same. But that is not the way to begin a review of his first book, for as it turns out I *am* very much impressed. As I think of *The Crow and the Heart*, I find myself believing not in its sustained power or concentration of language, but in a carefulness which bursts, once or twice or three times, into a kind of frenzied eloquence, a near-hysteria, and in these frightening places sloughing off a set of mannerisms which in the rest of the book seems determined to reduce Carruth to the level of a thousand other poets who can do, just as easily as he, most of the things he does in about three-fourths of these poems. Often, Carruth appears not to have learned the Gresham's Law of poetry, which states that the more sounds and images you crowd into a line, the less effect they have. He seldom lets you forget that you are reading something which has been written, and written again, and then written some more. These poems strike me as being completely mechanical and lifeless, with more than a hint of academic dilettantism about them. They are Suspect, and I for one, cannot take them seriously. The subjects of the poems are completely obscured in a blur of likely-sounding words.

This is the white king's palace: snowflakes flounce
On every draught, dally in secret aisles,

Bow and depart, an instant clap of fury,
And winds, O sparrow, shake your chandelier

That leaps and branches toward the reeling walls.

This is supposed to be a description of a snowfall, but it is a decorator's description, with a great deal more emphasis on the describing than on the snow, and so we get a little shimmer of words and no sense of winter at all. And the same thing happens over and over again.

What kind of thing, here where my mother's flowers
Bark colors only, like a tranced bazaar,
Is my late lingering love for you, which flows
Beyond all those events, past the Azores?

I guess (and I am only guessing) that " bark colors " is intended to indicate that the colors are raucous and irritating, and call attention to themselves mindlessly and unnecessarily. Actually, though, this is not what happens in the beholder's mind. He thinks momentarily only of a preposterous image of flowers like dogs, or like side-show barkers, and then dismisses it, his attention having been retained by neither flowers nor dogs. Because the objects which are called to our attention are vertiginously disembodied in language, considerable doubt is cast on the veracity and imagination of the mind that brought them up and presented them in this way. As Auden says, the poet's job is to find out the images " that hurt and connect," and a great many of Carruth's don't, at least not for me. They are like musical exercises that one wants to hear dissolve into the real playing.

The point where this happens is page 19, for those who wish to consult the text. " On a Certain Engagement South of Seoul " is as fine a poem as an American has ever written about the ex-soldier's feelings, and that takes in a lot of territory. It is only after the Inevitable has clamped us by the back of the neck that we go back and look carefully at the poem, and see that it is written in terza rima. And so, hushed and awed, we learn something about the power of poetic form, and the way in which it can both concentrate and release meaning, when meaning is present. This poem suggests, too, that Carruth is one of the poets (perhaps all poets are some of these poets) who write their best, pushing past limit after limit, only in the grip of recalling some overpowering experience. When he does not have such a subject at hand, Carruth amuses himself by being playfully skillful with internal rhyme, inventing bizarre Sitwellian images, being witty and professionally sharp. And there is much of this. But through Carruth's verses-by-anybody we are led slowly and a little restively, like the true mad, into "The Asylum," surely one of the most remarkable sequences of recent years. It is a low-keyed, extremely intelligent, tremblingly helpless poem about insanity and its terrible cure. It draws conclusions that no one but Carruth could have drawn, and which, by the miraculous process that takes place in poetry as good as this, manages also to speak for the rest of us, too, and for our society. I hope I am not making Carruth's powerful writing appear ordinary by talking about it as I do, but you must let him, and not me, convince you that it is neither. I should like very much to quote long stretches of "The Asylum," but I restrain myself in order to give the poem the chance it deserves of building up in the reader's mind as it was meant to. I suggest, then, that you buy Carruth's book and read "On a Certain Engagement," "The Fat Lady," and "The Asylum." They have done us proud.

The Crow and the Heart, by Hayden Carruth, Macmillan, 1960, $1.50.

II—*Journey To A Known Place*

Carruth's *Journey to a Known Place* is worth waiting for: a real event. I can only give an inadequate, betraying sketch of this beautifully conceived and imagined poem, into which Carruth blends his tremendous and sensitive vocabulary (surely the largest and most precise since Hart Crane's) with a mixture of cold, steady fury and nightmarish passion in the presence of which I can do little more than record my amazement and gratitude. Mr. Carruth's Known Place is the world itself, seen and experienced in and through its classic elements, earth, water, air, and fire. Each of its four sections begins with the protagonist's apprehension of one of the elements and follows him as he goes into it, comes to know it, lives it through a process of primal metamorphosis and then emerges in preparation for his entry into the next element, until all is resolved in fire. Since part of the immense force of the poem depends upon its closely-packed, slow-rolling diction over long stretches, quotation in brief can hardly do more than suggest its quality. But when Mr. Carruth's man-fish goes

> Down, down to the stiller mid-regions
> Where giant sea-snails hung torpid in copulation,
> Half out of their shells, white flesh rolling, exposed
> Obscenely in the slow coiling and cramping of a cruel
> And monstrously deliberate ecstasy

we have had a vision of the blind and necessary horror of nature which is, for my money, very nearly absolute.

Like his man-bird, Mr. Carruth is " skilled now in the/ profound and lovely/necessities," and his wonderful new poem, which begins with a huddle of refugees and ends in the City of the Sun, is bound to be discussed and reread for many years. *Journey to a Known Place* is a painful and magnificent poem; it really hurts and it really sings,

71

and I can only urge readers to buy it and live with it, even though New Directions has put it on the market at $12.50, a price that will unfortunately keep many readers away from what would certainly be a profound and moving experience.

Journey to a Known Place, by Hayden Carruth, New Directions, 1961, $12.50.

RANDALL JARRELL

A. Why are we Two?

B. I find that my opinions of Randall Jarrell's poetry are so violent that I have summoned you, or created you, out of niggling and Opposing Winds, to furnish me with arguments against which my own will stand forth even stronger, which I should like them to do.

A. I am glad you have created me. I think it good for writers to have the most violent possible arguments brought into play against them. Even unfair arguments. If the work is strong enough, all these will be overcome. Now, I was moved by Jarrell's poems even when I was Wind. Now that I am a Voice therefrom, I find I am moved even more, for I am nearer the human things he writes about.

B. I take it, then, that I have brought forth a satisfactory Opposing Self, for you seem to like Jarrell's poems.

A. I do. I think his book is, or should certainly be, the occasion of a Triumph. He has been writing for twenty years now, and this book contains a fair portion of all he will do as a writer: that is, the book is a monument, if not to Jarrell *in toto*, then at least to his " early phase," no matter what he may do later.

B. And why is the book a Triumph, may I ask?

A. Because it is the work of an honest, witty, intelligent, and deeply gifted man, a man who knows more about poetry, and knows it in better, more human ways, than any other of our time. If you add to these other things that he has a rare poetic intelligence which works, not for itself, but totally in the service of human beings, in compassion and love, then you will have an idea of the kind of Triumph I'm talking about. All you can do about a book

73

like this, as Herbert Read said of Dylan Thomas's *Deaths And Entrances,* is to praise it.

B. I must tell you, then, that to me the book is dull beyond all dullness of stupefaction or petrifaction; that when I read it from end to end I know more of boredom than the dead do. " In plain American that dogs and cats can read " the poems are the most untalentedly sentimental, self-indulgent, and insensitive writings that I can remember; when I read them I cry and laugh helplessly all night, over the reputation that has come out of such stuff.

A. I would say, in answer, that you have missed the entire point of Jarrell's contribution, which is that of writing about real things, rather than playing games with words. He is set like a kind of laughing death against the technique-on-principle people that fill the quarterlies. His world is the World, and People, and not the cultivated island of books, theories, and schools. Can't you see that?

B. Would you give me an example of this attitude at work in one of Jarrell's poems?

A. I'll just pick up a random sample. This is from " The Night Before the Night Before Christmas." He speaks of " the big old houses, the small new houses." Don't you see . . .

B. That's real enough, all right, if that's what you mean by real. That is, there *are* big old houses and small new houses, and perhaps this observation tells us something about the economic and social changes that have taken place in the time between the building of the two types of houses. But isn't the statement pretty much of a commonplace? After all, we don't need a poet to point this out to us. Am I to believe that you and Jarrell think that comment of this rather tame and obvious kind constitutes Triumphal Poetry? I should be sorry to think so.

A. You certainly *are* to believe it. It is, for instance, far more important than surrealist poems, or those of Garcia Lorca's "Poet in New York," or any other poetry that uses

74

objects as counters to whirl into and out of bizarre images, simply for the sake of the images, and the bizarreness. Jarrell's poems are far too respectful of experience, of life as it is lived by people, for that to happen. Their world is our world.

B. Now this word " real " : Hadn't we better examine it a little more closely ? Is it actually as important as you say to Jarrell's writing ?

A. It *is* his writing. He writes about the things we know; that is, he writes about cats, common soldiers, about the dilemmas of children, and . . . and the small man, the man " things are done to," usually by the State, to the man's almost willing detriment and slow consternation.

B. " Reality," though, is what, exactly ? The philosophers have gone into cold graves, for ages, still arguing about the nature of Reality, and probably will do so forever. Do you mean to tell me that if I read Jarrell's poems " in the right spirit " I will have the answer to all these vexing questions the Ages have turned back from with only provisional, unsatisfactory solutions ?

A. Yes; in a sense, you will. Like any poet's, Jarrell's is an experiential reality. I believe that, without becoming entangled in metaphysics, we can assume that his reality is " the common ground of experience " of twentieth century man, especially the American, but not confined to him. Through poems about what has happened to this man (or to his child) in this time, we get, in an extremely detailed, moving, and " true " way the experience of our time defined. And that is Reality enough.

B. " Reality," then, is what everybody knows and feels it is, since we all have roughly the same experiences as human beings living under (approximately) the same conditions. When there is a war, for instance, we all react to it.

A. That's right.

B. And you think that it's important that Jarrell appeals to others' participation in this common ground of experience: that his poems draw their strength at least in part from this appeal?

A. I do. Can you deny that you have undergone many of the things he writes about?

B. No. I have undergone them. But so have newspapers, mediocre movies, soap operas, and bad poems. So has my old Aunt Virgie, on television. It is not enough that the poet's world be that of " all of us." Of course he must begin there, but that fact doesn't make him a poet, or his writings valuable.

A. Nobody is asserting anything of that kind. You oversimplify much too drastically.

B. Jarrell himself seems to assume something of this nature, though. In his criticism he speaks frequently, even obsessively, of a poet's evoking not " a " but " the " real world; he says of Whitman's world that it " so plainly *is* the world " (italics Jarrell's), and so on.

A. You are still missing the point. The poet must evoke a world that is realler than real: his work must result in an intensification of qualities, you might say, that we have all observed and lived, but the poet has observed and lived most deeply of all. This world is so real that the experienced world is transfigured and intensified, through the poem, into itself, a deeper itself, a more characteristic itself. If a man can make words do this, he is a poet. Only men who can do this are poets.

B. Isn't it, though, what all poets are trying to do? Or at least half of them, anyway. There are some poets who are on the side of the World against Art, like Jarrell, and there are others, like the surrealists, Mallarmé, and

Valéry, who are for Art against the World. Nietzsche said that no true artist would tolerate for an instant the world as it is. Some artists want to characterize the world, and some to change it and make use of it in their own ways. Assuming for the moment that I, like you and Jarrell, think that the world ought to be characterized, let me ask you an important question: does Jarrell's work in fact do this intensifying and typifying you claim for it?

A. You bet it does. His realm is one of pity and terror, of a kind of non-understanding understanding (which I'll explain later), and above all of helplessness. All his people, the wounded soldiers, the children, the cancer patients, all these are people in predicaments that happen all the time. They are the things that our situation as human beings can't help bringing to bear on us. It is through the kind of compulsion that these things force up in us that Jarrell writes his poems. He is saying, in almost every poem, " There is no explanation for what is happening to you. I don't understand why it is; I can tell you nothing. But I know how it must be for you." The poems are moving in the way life is, when these things happen in it. And there is the compassion of a man in them, a man who knows that his helpless pity won't do any good, won't change anything, but who keeps pouring it out anyway because he can't help it. There is your real helplessness, and there is your poet Jarrell. And if you read him in a little less cynical manner than you have done, you would know this; you would become fully Human.

B. But these are *poems* he is trying to write. If you ignore that, you substitute sentimentality and special pleading (admirable though it be) for the poet's true work, which is to put down words in a certain order. You get, in fact, *my* Jarrell. Tell me, my Compassionate friend, with all these fine things that happen to you

77

when you read a Jarrell poem, can you honestly tell me that you think Jarrell has a good ear, or is very perceptive or even accurate in his use of language?

A.   Yes, I think he has, and is, in an unexceptional, unobtrusive way.

B.   (reads)
    The yaks groaning with tea, the burlaps
    Lapping and lapping each stunned universe . . .
Now, how about those " burlaps/Lapping and lapping "? What put that one past him if not laxity and not-hearing? Come, now; has he really the poet's deep, instinctive feel of language, the sense of language as a *mode* of experience?

A.   He has, but he has a more important commitment, which is to humanity. And that is better.

B.   Not in poetry, it isn't. Language and experience have got to be interactive at a deeper (or higher) level to make poetry happen. Deeper or higher than Jarrell commands, I mean. I maintain that Jarrell doesn't have in more than the slightest and rather synthetic and predictable degree this kind of grasp on language. He has a good sense of the poetically profitable situation, which by itself is by no means enough. It won't do, when you write a bad poem, a poem that doesn't " raise to consciousness " (to paraphrase Collingwood) a given segment of experience, to say, " Well, the World told me to say it that way. I looked at the Thing, the War, the Child, the Wounded Man, and it looked back, and the World told me, ' Son, what you see, *is*.' And so I put it down without Artifice, or with only a little, and I felt Compassion for the subject, and I had a poem. And that's what poetry is, by gum." No; that won't wash. Let Jarrell write a single phrase that has the harnessed verbal energy of Valéry's " La mer, la mer, toujours recommencée " and I'll begin to see him as a poet. And let me add that that line, as far as I'm concerned, has more of " the World " in it than all of Jarrell's; it has because the poet has put it there.

In Jarrell's poems, the " Real World " is far too often merely called on, and not created at all, by descriptions that would not be remarkable in an ordinary naturalistic short-story or novel. This is in part the case, I suppose, because Jarrell evidently considers it a particular virtue, in his espousal of the " real," to cling like death to the commonplace, as though the Real were only the Ordinary, after all, and the solution that artists have sought for centuries were resolved in that recognition. But when Garcia Lorca says, " Your belly is a battle of roots," is that Ordinary ?

A. Jarrell might not admit it as poetry.

B. I can't judge as to that. But *I* admit it. Furthermore, it seems to me to be almost fearfully " real," Jarrell be damned. It comes down to this: I don't think you can impose your own notion of " reality " as everyone's, no matter how much you assume and take for granted that everyone is like you, or should be like you. You can't legitimately offer your personal interpretation of " reality " as though it were universally acceptable, and write criticism and poetry out of an agreement with yourself that this is the case.

A. I suppose I am at liberty to believe in Jarrell's as a real world, as a world that is probably as near as a poet can bring me to the World, whatever that is (but I *feel* it !).

B. You are. Realler, though, than Dylan Thomas's ?

A. Well, yes. Not so good, though, as poetry. But Jarrell's world is nearer what I know.

B. How about what Thomas knows ? You appear to be willing to accept this business of Ordinariness as Reality. Tell me, then, why you believe Thomas's to be the better poetry?

A. He does something, well, something *else* to the world. Changes it, maybe.

B. Yes; birds fly through water, stars burst out of bearing mothers' ears (this from the prose), hunchbacks turn into tall young women, and so on. He plays pretty fast and loose with your Ordinary Reality, doesn't he?

A. Yes, I guess so. But what you're saying is that anyone who plays fast and loose with things is thereby a poet, which is just as untrue as any of the assumptions you say Jarrell makes.

B. I don't intend that inference at all. Would you admit that Thomas's successes depend at least in part on these qualities of changing and shaping?

A. Yes, and so would Jarrell, probably. He says of Whitman that he is "the rashest, the most inexplicable and unlikely—the most impossible, one wants to say—of poets." Doesn't that knock out almost everything you've said?

B. Not at all. Consider the kinds of individualities he thinks relevant to poetry. All, or almost all the poets he likes, Frost, Williams, Elizabeth Bishop, Robert Lowell, Corbière, even poets mentioned, as it were, in passing, like Adam Drinan and Niccolo degli Albizzi, have what qualities in common?

A. I should say (except possibly of Lowell) that they use simple diction, different kinds of unpoetical off-handness, and are preoccupied largely with . . .

B. Everyday objects, scenes, and so on: brooms, cats, garbage cans, broccoli patches, chickens, squirrels, rabbit-hutches, socks, boxes. If someone has a simile comparing defeated soldiers to " . . . barrels rolling, jolting," Jarrell will be more likely to approve it than if the soldiers were likened to dispossessed kings, unless the kings were homey ones. But mightn't kings be more effective, in some conceivable instances?

A. Aren't you just assuming all this?

B. I don't think I am, entirely. Most of the metaphors Jarrell cites as good are of this type. Almost all of his own are. " His raft's hot-water-bottle weight," for instance. There are hundreds. If you make a metaphor, Jarrell seems to be telling you, the second term of it, the thing the first term is being compared to, must be something homey, something ordinary, or else you are not dealing with " reality " and therefore not writing poetry.

A. Are you asserting that poetry shouldn't or can't be made with these things?

B. Of course not. Only that it can be made with other things as well.

A. Tell me, do you think these objections hold true of the war poems?

B. Yes, more even than of the others, if that is possible. They have all the attitudes that most people think ought to be shown by poets during wars. Can you imagine a poet loving war, or not pitying the individual soldiers?

A. Does that prevent Jarrell from really pitying them?

B. No, and he does pity them. I am disturbed, though, that despite all the pity he shows, none of it is actually brought to bear on any*one*. Did Jarrell never love any *person* in the service with him? Did he just pity himself and all the Others, in a kind of monstrous, abstract, complacent, and inhuman Compassion? I don't think there are really any *people* in the war poems. There are only The Ball Turret Gunner, A Pilot from the Carrier, The Wingman, and assorted faceless types in uniform. They are just collective Objects, or Attitudes, or Killable Puppets. You care very little what happens to them, and that is terrible.

A. It seems to me that Jarrell is writing mostly *about* the impersonal side of war: about the fact that wars are fought, now, almost entirely by machines, and that men suffer more or less as an irrelevant afterthought of the machines.

B. Yes, but men, not Man, suffer. You do get, however, in Jarrell's war poems, some sense of this vast and impersonal aspect of modern warfare, but little of it is realized dramatically. Most of the stuff about aircraft carriers, for instance, is like watching a good film on the subject, like "The Fighting Lady." If I had to choose between the film and the poems, I would choose the film. I can think of no film I would prefer to Thomas's "Ceremony After a Fire Raid." Jarrell's second-hand Reality simply does not do enough. His work is just sophisticated journalism; it is craft, in Collingwood's definition: working up a predictable emotion, and damned poor metrically, too. In these later poems, do you suppose Jarrell cares, any more, that poetry is supposed to display at least some degree of rhythmic concentration?

A. He is *beyond* those considerations. He is not Yvor Winters, you know. He is not your mechanical stress-monger. He is a Man, as he says in the last line of the book. He has broken away from all that petty finger-and-toe-counting, those neat, rectangular stanzas. He is past being concerned with those mechanics. He has attained a realm "where only necessary things are done,/With that supreme and grave dexterity that ignores technique" (though I may be misquoting from Kirkup here, in a word or two).

B. You say he's "broken through" these things, that he knows enough, now, not to have to worry about technical matters. Yet it seems to me that he hasn't

82

really reached them at all, in any significant way, or has fallen progressively away from the very slight acquaintance with them evidenced in his first book. The unstated and insistent principle underlying the later poems is "The situation is enough." But, as I keep saying, he has not the power, or the genius, or the talent, or the inclination, or whatever, to make experience rise to its own most intense, concentrated, and meaningful level, a level impossible without *that* poet's having caught it in *those* words. And there the matter rests, as far as I'm concerned.

A. I can see that there's no arguing with you. But I believe that Randall Jarrell will have something to say to people for a very long time to come, especially as the world tries increasingly to survive by inhumanity (assuming you agree with me on this). The poems give you the feel of a time, our time, as no other poetry of our century does, or could, even. They put on your face, nearer than any of your own looks, more irrevocably than your skin, the uncomprehending stare of the individual caught in the State's machinery: in an impersonal, invisible, man-made, and uncontrollable Force. They show in front of you a child's slow, horrified, magnificently un-understanding and growing loss of innocence in which we all share and can't help: which we can neither understand nor help in ourselves in the hands of the State any more than can the children in our hands. The poems are one long look, through this expression, into a child's face, as the Things of modern life happen around it, happen to it, so that you see the expressions change, and even feel the breath change over you, and you come to be aware that you are staring back in perfect and centered blindness, in which everything to pity is clear as death, and none of the reasons for any of it. Now *that* is our time. It is humanity in

83

the twentieth century. Or whatever is good, worth saving, there. And that is your poet Randall Jarrell, to stand against any objections, even legitimate ones. He gives you, as all great or good writers do, a foothold in a realm where literature itself is inessential, where your own world is more yours than you could ever have thought, or even felt, but is one you have always known.

Selected Poems, by Randall Jarrell, Knopf, 1955, $4.00.

E. E. CUMMINGS

When you judge one of E. E. Cummings' books, you have to judge them all; you have to judge Cummings. Perhaps this is true to some degree of reviewing all poets, but it is entirely true in Cummings' case. His books are all exactly alike, and one is faced with evaluating Cummings as a poet, using the current text simply as a hitherto unavailable source of quotations. Let me make my own position clear right away. I think that Cummings is a daringly original poet, with more virility and more sheer, uncompromising talent than any other living American writer. I cannot and would not want to deny, either, that he dilutes even the finest of his work with writing that is hardly more than the defiant playing of a child, though the fact that he does this with the superb arrogance of genius has always seemed to me among the most attractive of his qualities. I love Cummings' verse, even a great deal of it that is not lovable or even respectable, but it is also true that I am frequently and thoroughly bored by its continuous attitudinizing and its dogmatic preaching. I have often felt that there must be something hiddenly wrong with his cult of spontaneity and individuality, that these attributes have to be insisted upon to the extent to which Cummings insists on them. I feel, also, that " love " and the other well-known emotions that Cummings tirelessly espouses are being imposed on me categorically, and that I stand in some danger of being shot if I do not, just at that moment, wish to love someone or pick a rose or lean against a tree watching the snow-flakes come down. The famous mannerisms, too: aren't they, by now, beginning to pall pretty heavily? Were some of them, even when they were new, worth very much? I can, for example, think of no two literary devices which interest me less than the countless " un "-words Cummings is fond of using, and his wearisome, cute, and mechanical substitution of other parts of speech for nouns (" a which of slim of blue/of here will who/straight up into the where . . ."). Yet when you come on a passage like this, what can you feel but silence, gratitude, and rejoicing?

> now air is air and thing is thing: no bliss
> of heavenly earth beguiles our spirits, whose
> miraculously disenchanted eyes
> live the magnificent honesty of space.

Here is something entirely beautiful, with the odd, arresting, directness-from-another-angle that characterizes the best poetry, and can change your life. One thinks of Blake's observation about the crooked roads without improvement, and is glad of the quotation, and even more glad that Cummings has lived along those roads with vitality and constancy, and has defended them against the cheapjacks of life and of the word with the belligerency and the withering scorn he has. A few years ago, reviewing Cummings' *Poems 1923-1954* in *The New York Times Book Review,* Randall Jarrell deplored Cummings' insistence on his difference from other men. Whether or not Cummings does this to the extent Mr. Jarrell suggests, and I think he does, I am more delighted than dismayed by it. Just this jealous treasuring of his individuality, his uniqueness, has enabled Cummings' personality to flower in a number of perfectly inimitable poems, and in countless passages in other poems beside which the efforts of all but a few other contemporary poets pale into competent indifference. It has encouraged also, I suppose, the various devices and mannerisms for which Cummings is celebrated. The important thing, however, is that Cummings has felt the need, and followed it, of developing absolutely in his own way, of keeping himself and his writing whole,

86

preferring to harbor his most grievous and obvious faults quite as if they were part and parcel of his most original and valuable impulses, which perhaps they are. The poems in *95 Poems* are no better and no worse than Cummings' best and worst poems in his other books, though the percentage of good poems over bad is considerably higher here than is customary. As always, Cummings is his own most distinguished and devastating parodist, able with penetrating wit to hold his own work up to the ridicule some of it deserves, and then, in the next poem, or even in the next line, to restore it to an eminence which seals the critic's mouth and changes him into a more perceptive being than he has been since his fifth year. But how is this done? I attempted to answer this question by doing my best to determine which of the two or three writers present in Cummings I admire most. It is certainly not the one who depends on a number of elementary and quite predictable tricks of typography to make points which could be made more easily, and probably more effectively, by other means. In Cummings' experiments in breaking up words and using syllables in various permutations and combinations on the page, I have only the faintest interest.

> l (a
>
> le
>
> af
>
> fa
>
> ll
>
> s)
>
> one
>
> l
>
> iness

There is not much doubt as to what the vertical arrangement of the letters, here, is meant to do. Within the enveloping context of " loneliness," the motion of the leaf, set parenthetically, the initially unexplained "1" which completes the key word when one goes back to it, all show pretty well how this device in Cummings' poems usually operates. Although this treatment (one can hardly call it a technique) has, in addition to a simple kind of puzzle-interest, the slight advantage of approximating kinaesthetically the falling of the leaf, and of literally surrounding it with the human emotion which it connotes or causes, I cannot for the life of me think of this piece as particularly good poetry, or particularly good anything; certainly I do not think of it in the same way I do of some of Cummings' poems. No; I am most drawn to the Cummings whose quirky, indignant sharpness of observation produced the unforgettable pages dealing with Jean le Nègre in *The Enormous Room*, over which no type-setter asked for a raise or cut his throat: to the writer whose fantastic and uncompromising devotion to a spontaneous, outward-going (and typically American, if we would just *be* Americans) view of the world permeates his prose and most of his poems with gorgeous, unpremeditated energy: to the Cummings whose entirely personal daring with diction and image brings us into a Chaplinesque, half-comic, half-holy reconciliation with the events through which we live. His excesses are, most certainly, enormous, as one feels they should be in a genuine poet. Cummings is without question one of the most insistent and occasionally one of the most successful users of pathetic fallacy in the history of the written word. He is one of the most blatant sentimentalists, one of the most absurdly and grandly over-emotional of poets, one of the flimsiest thinkers, and one of the truly irreplaceable sensibilities that we have known, with the blind, irresistible devotion to his exact perceptions, to his way of knowing and doing, and to his personal and incorruptible relation to the English language that an authentic poet must have.

Immediacy and intensity are Cummings' twin gods, and he has served them with a zeal and single-mindedness which we should learn to appreciate even more fully as these traits tend to disappear from our verse, giving way, as they seem to be doing, to a more withdrawn, philosophical, "considered," and altogether safer point of view. I can think of no other qualities so much needed in contemporary poetry as those which Cummings has spent his life discovering ways to make viable. Whether or not successful in every instance, all of Cummings' skill, so special to himself that we cannot imagine anyone else making use of it, has gone to establish and consecrate the moment: the event which is taking place *now*: the thing which will never be repeated in quite this same way, and which, quite likely, would ordinarily not even be noticed as it happens. Cummings' several devices are always means by which to get at this, and to show "what happens" in its pure, inexplicable, purposeless instancy and intensity: in its meaning-beyond-meaning. He has never felt the need to broaden his subject-matter, or to systematize its implications, or even to notice anything beyond the experiences and scenes which attain the highest degree of intuitive meaning for *him*: love, love with sex, sex without love, spring, flowers, snow, death, sunlight, moonlight, leaves, birds, his family, hatred of money and money-makers and public figures. No one would insist that Cummings be a more systematic thinker than he is, because of his spectacular success in feeling responsively and deeply and verbally, but I for one often wish, when reading his poems, that they had somewhat more intellectual structure or firmness under them. I had as well withdraw that statement, though, for poems 48 and 49 in this book are wonderful poems, and are so quite without taking any notice whatever of my objections. Aside from his big *Poems 1923-1954*, this is Cummings' best book; there are so many good things in it that to begin to quote whole poems would necessitate my going on for pages. As a reviewer, I note this with relief, for to point out all the brilliant passages would entail having to indicate ludicrous failures also, and with having to reckon again with the fact that Cummings has long since passed (perhaps with his first poem, perhaps when he was born) the point where writing correctly, well or badly according to other lights than his own, made the slightest difference to him. He is so strongly of a piece that the commentator feels ashamed and even a little guilty in picking out flaws, as though he were asked to call attention to the aesthetic defects in a rose. It is better to say what must finally be said about Cummings: that he has helped to give life to the language, for language is renewed by the best perceptions of its most valuably intuitive and devoted users, and by no other means. Cummings belongs in the class of poets who have done this, not by virtue of his tinkering with typography, but because of his superior insight into the fleeting and eternal moments of existence: not because of words broken up into syllables and strewn carefully about the page, but because of right words with other right words, which say what they do whether they are upside down, right-side up, inside out, backward, or any other way.

>   to stand (alone) in some
>   autumnal afternoon:
>   breathing a fatal
>   stillness . . .

Cummings is an important poet because he has insisted, by virtue of his fine, irascible talent, on the primacy of the perpetually-happening, never-repeated " natural miracle," and on our feeling with what we see, and seeing with what we feel, spontaneously, thoughtlessly, and totally. I do not in the least mean to slight his typographical innovations, which may well be of greater import than I have been willing to concede; I only wish to reiterate that what I consider Cummings' finest moments are dependent not on these innovations, such as they are, but on combinations of words that deliver the necessary insights regardless of what splintering process may or may not take place among them. These poems, such as "Paris: this April sunset completely utters," and "Always before your voice my soul," show that part or perhaps most of the miracle is in our observing and responding: that it is we who must do the seeing and feeling, unashamedly and faithful to nothing but our actual responses. In poems as strongly charged with as unforeseeable and as unique a personality as Cummings', that is a very great deal.

95 Poems, by E. E. Cummings, Harcourt, Brace, 1958, $4.00.

91

ELDER OLSON

To my untutored mind, which probably shouldn't be allowed an opinion of this sort, Elder Olson has always appeared the most gifted of the influential University of Chicago "neo-Aristotelian" school of literary aesthetics. From time to time he publishes a few poems, too. I have come to watch eagerly for these, and have noted with especial delight their difference from the complicated and rarefied trafficking with universals that he and his colleagues do in the pages of the learned journals. All of Olson's poems that I have seen are in his new book, together with five short plays which are witty, ingenious, and amusing, but which are not up to even the lesser of the poems in originality and lasting effectiveness. The plays are marred by excessive reliance on literary "gimmicks" and surprises, and do not impress me as being anything more than mildly successful, even within their modest intentions. "Faust," for example, is a humanist parable on the old story, but with the twist that Faust, in quest of youth instead of knowledge, is taken at his word in an entirely different sense from that which he intended, becomes the victim of a purely scientific retribution, and is made to suffer "regressive evolution" back to the state of the primates, and beyond. "The Illusionists" makes use of Huxleyan "illusion machines" which the populace of the earth, habituated for years to illusions by other means such as television, the cinema, and advertising, eagerly adopts, because "real individual happiness is incompatible with the good of the State; besides, it isn't possible." Men no longer see any reason to distinguish reality from illusion, and embrace the illusion machines even though they must pay the machine-masters with their flesh. As may be inferred, these five small plays are exclusively dramas of ideas, with the characters simply serving as a number of stand-ins for various points of view. Once the surprise-packages of their denouements have been opened, they come to seem contrived and a little thin.

The poems are in another class altogether. Obvious influences there are, to be sure, and not all of them good; to note one, the well-known " Ballad of the Scarecrow Christ " is disastrously in the shadow of Dylan Thomas's " Ballad of the Long-legged Bait " :

> Look, look! Amid what pomp of water
> He lordly rides like the light of day;
> All the sea-robed waves throng round,
> Sea-foam garlands all his way . . .

This is not Olson's best manner. But " Crucifix," " The Jack-in-the-box," and, above all, " A Nocturnal For His Children " are models of difficult thinking made profoundly clear, and of a power of organization which brings the Great Questions into perfectly convincing rapport with the actual circumstances of everyday life. I am delighted and even awestruck by Olson's capacity to assemble the materials of his poems around the ideas they dramatize, and by the ease with which he wields his verse-forms upon basic and eternal considerations, steadily and evenly.

> Not in God's image was man
> First created, but in
> Likeness of a beast;
> Until that beast became man,
> All travailled in death and pain
> And shall travail still
> Till man be the image of God
> And nothing shall transform
> Man to that image but love;
> And this I believe is God's will.

And all shall work that Will:
Planet and planet shall spin,
Atom and atom, until
The scriptures of heaven and earth
Mountain and ocean, spell
The one unnameable Name
Of One we know nothing of,
Save what we learn from love . . .

Reading this, and many other poems and parts of poems in Olson's book, I keep asking myself why his work is not better known. I can think of no adequate answer, and must leave Olson's relative neglect a mystery, trusting I have done what I could to rectify what seems to me a really unfortunate situation, and hoping to enlist the aid of Time.

Plays and Poems, 1948-58, by Elder Olson, University of Chicago Press, 1958, $4.00.

RICHARD EBERHART

Richard Eberhart has long been an enigma for critics, and doubtless will be so forever. To make things even harder for us, he has all but perfected a number of devices that he employs, cleverly and with increasing skill, to hide the fact that he is one of the most authentically gifted and instinctively poetic minds of our time. If we must choose, and in this case it begins to look as if we must, between the merely formal and un-inspired and the unformed and talented—if we cannot have executive form *and* inspiration—we will choose the latter: we will choose Eberhart over Robert Bridges or Howard Baker. That much is or should be plain. Yet Eberhart is often irritating beyond belief; in this book he has indulged himself increasingly in a mannerism which first began to be obtrusive in *Undercliff*: a gabby, jocularly pedantic dialect, largely of his own invention, packed with awkward and ponderously frivolous word-play like "the election of erection" and "Enrapture my blessing/Immediacy of perception." One might imagine the heights to which an untrammelled and en-thusiastic use of this procedure might take American poetry, but one does not have to imagine them; they are all reached in *Great Praises*: surely it is hard to believe any of us will ever see again, at least in the book of a sometime superior poet, anything quite like "Super-abundant/Faculty manifests sun-burned rarity/As he eschews aridity and valley." It is an irony with aspects of the fabulous that Eberhart's main pre-occupation as a poet—the achievement of true "immediacy of per-ception"—is made literally impossible by the heap of ill-digested bookish language he uses to try to persuade you that he is, too, writing from the center of the place "where everything is seen in its purity." Without this manner, on the other hand, Eberhart speaks with utter conviction and directness.

> I wanted to give him some gift,
> Small child dying slowly,
> With brave blue intelligent eyes,
> His form withered piteously.
>
> Only in the intelligence of those eyes
> Where life had retreated for a piercing look
> Was the enormous mystery justified,
> As he inhaled the betraying oxygen.

I don't know whether or not this kind of clairvoyant simplicity would be available to Eberhart if it were not for the unnatural and frequently ludicrous excesses of the other poems. I am willing to suppose that it would not, though surely his seems a strange route to take toward the first and only poetic Innocence. Yet there are wonderfully exciting times in which Eberhart does appear to be able to make of himself " flesh without a mind," and to speak with penetrating and involving spontaneity, and we must therefore grant him whatever means he adjudges favorable to such states, for at these times we recognize him for what he assuredly is: one of the writers who are opening up the world to our life, from the inside.

Great Praises, by Richard Eberhart, Oxford, 1957, $4.00.

BROTHER ANTONINUS

Reviewing religious poets, determinedly religious ones, always makes me a little nervous. I feel somewhat as if I were reviewing God, and am intimidated at flying in the face of all that good will with the mere instruments of my own taste and judgment. This is especially true when I came to Brother Antoninus. I remember him from several years back as William Everson, who wrote some of the first poetry I ever truthfully liked. Along with his new book, I went back and read his old one, *The Residual Years*, and found it full of the hatred and necessity of sex, and of a very convincing and powerful, from-inside-the-thing feeling about California farmers and farming.

> Deep sun, deep sky;
> No wind now for the dance of the leaves,
> But the light clean on the shape of the neck;
> And the deep sound of the heart.

Everson is (or was) best in simple, tactile description. His poems in *The Residual Years* are unforced and open, and I renewed my acquaintance with many of them gladly, noting their imperfections and setting them aside in favor of the living quality that these pieces give off. And yet I was also struck, as I had been before, by the author's humorless, even owlish striving after self-knowledge and certainty, his intense and bitter inadequacy and frustration. I suppose I should have known, when I first read him fourteen years ago, that these problems would be resolved in religious orthodoxy, though I could not have guessed that Everson himself would become Brother Antoninus in the Catholic Church. In *The Crooked Lines of God* I encountered a good deal less of what I am pleased to call poetry than in *The Residual Years*, though if there were any justice there would be more. The verse here is of the kind I had hoped not to find: page after page of not-very-good, learned, dry sermonizing which in several places leans toward an attitude which I cannot help believing is somewhat self-righteous and even self-congratulatory. Before the poems proper ever begin, it is disconcerting to hear a writer say that what follows is "tortured between grace and the depraved human heart," as though he were presenting his poems, not as the tentative, hopeful ventures that all poems must be, but as a confident course from the mere estate of being human to the extreme Beatification. He talks of "my new poetic vision" as though it were an irrefutable fact. But alas, it is not so. What Brother Antoninus offers, instead of the "vision" he speaks of, is a sober, unimaginative forthrightness and a nagging insistence that he is right and you are, no matter what *else* you may believe, wrong. What I find peculiarly disagreeable in Brother Antoninus' work is his basic dislike of people and of sex, and this seems to me to be based at least as much on secular reasons as on religious, especially considering the fact that he shows the same distastes in *The Residual Years*, though there they are offered simply as personal feelings instead of Enlightenment. It may be that I am being unfair to Brother Antoninus, and if so I hope he will forgive me. Nevertheless, I still must say that the material offered here is much nearer to being apologetics than poetry. Worse; the author's determination to make his subjects as important and impressive as he believes they should be only succeeds in puffing them up into unbelievability.

> Good Peter, upside down,
> Straddles the Roman sun,

His legs like aqueducts
Bloody the down-hung head.
Already here the packed arena fills;
Its martyrs mount their yardarms.
The starveling lion
Snuffs the blood-stung air,
And the maiden's coif
Mats the tiger's jaw.
All, all are here. Their pain
Reaches already to this swollen Heart
That lugs and labors like a giant sea
Clasping its wounded islands,
Toning its solemn note upon that shore,
To weep out its geologic woe alone.

Unfortunately, as I have said before, the means, risks, and results of poetry are the same for religious verse as they are for any other kind. Hopkins knew this, and he labored mightily to see what the world had to show him. If inspiration is religious, and is also inspiration, the result will be good religious poetry, provided the words are adequate to express it. If the writing is religious in theme, but without the spark that only imagination can supply, the result will be much like the verse of Brother Antoninus and Thomas Merton, all argument, good intentions, and no light. It is too bad that, in verse coming to us from intensely devout, serious, and dedicated men, we get enough solemn, dead metaphors to fill the stuffed owl's mouth for generations to come, enough laborious theology to make us wish Thomas Merton were still an undergraduate Bohemian, and Brother Antoninus still a farmer in the San Joaquin Valley, ploughing God's land with his horses.

The Crooked Lines of God, by Brother Antoninus, University of Detroit Press, 1960, $4.00.

TOWARD A SOLITARY JOY

GARY SNYDER

Somehow it isn't enough, anymore, that there are
plenty of good poems around, as there are. What we
feel we need now is a poetry good in a way we could
not have foreseen: a kind of perceiving and writing
which will transcend and destroy our present criteria,
open new areas of experience, and release us to our own
waiting, hidden potentialities. Not that there haven't
been several tries. The "Movement" in England was
one, but it has come to surprisingly little. The carefully off-hand, self-effacing, intelligently embarrassed
tone so fashionable among young British poets a few
years ago now appears to have been only a cultivated
way of admitting imaginative bankruptcy. In this
country, the "Beats" are, of course, the nearest thing
we have to a poetry movement. Though, despite my
best efforts, I can't take most Beat poetry seriously, its
very existence shows that the well-bred verse of the
Schoolmen which dominated the forties and early fifties
is exhausted. As a consequence of these developments,
every book we read nowadays can be placed in one of
three categories, and by means of such placement we
can make a fairly accurate guess as to what the writer
believes our poetry should be. There are those who
assume that academic poetry is as good now as it was
in the forties and fifties, when almost nothing else was
printed, those who are convinced that academic poetry
is dead, and are trying energetically to bury it (the
Beats), and those who find themselves in a curious half-
way house between academic poetry and Somewhere
Else: Beatnikism, or their own hesitantly emerging and
personal vision of the New. This last place is where
Galway Kinnell, for example, is starting life.

The best of them, Gary Snyder, is not. I don't know

precisely what his relation to the Beats may be, but he is usually published with them, and has certainly taken up a good many of their preoccupations, such as Zen and the rest of the mail-order orientalism of the West Coast crowd. But he is also by far the most interesting of these poets that I have read. What you see about him immediately is his debt to the Pound of the *Cantos*: Pound's fragmented, juxtaposing method, his quotations (with and without quotation marks), and even his irritating use of the ampersand. But what you also see is that this is unmistakably the right technique for Mr. Snyder to use. The Pound style, at the same time so style-conscious and so styleless, can be very bad: disorganized, flat, pretentious, obscure, inconsequential, bookish, and dull. But in Mr. Snyder's work it is none of these. It is, instead, close to what Pound probably thinks it should be: sharp-edged, vivid, detached, concentrated both on the thing shown (the image) and on bringing it into a field of interpretation not explicitly given but formulated by the various quotations woven into the writing. The musing, drifting series of terse, observant statements does fix Snyder's experiences and beliefs in such a manner that they become available for us to live among and learn from. And that is the kind of living and learning—within another's life—that we are always hoping poetry will make possible.

Myths and Texts, by Gary Snyder, Totem Press (New York), 1960, $1.25.

GALWAY KINNELL

I like Galway Kinnell's poems mainly for their whole-hearted commitment to themselves, and for what I can only call their innocence. Mr. Kinnell cares quite openly and honestly about almost everything he has ever seen, heard of, or read about, and finds it rather easy to say so. There is nothing very tragic or tearing about him, or nothing very intense, either. He seems to me a natural poet: humanly likeable, gentle, ruminative. But he is disheart-eningly prolix. Prolixity is, of course, the foremost and perhaps only natural enemy of the natural poet, and Mr. Kinnell is going to have to do battle with it if he is to realize himself. Some of these pieces are almost too trivial to be believed, and even the best of them keep blurring into each other, since there is no real division, nothing to individualize them, make them separately ex-perienceable. They are just part of the amiable weather of the book. Poetry can do better than this, and so can Kinnell. The last long poem, " The Avenue Bearing the Initial of Christ into the New World," has some beautiful lines about such unbeautiful objects as carp in grocers' tanks and vegetable pushcarts. Here, you feel quite strongly a genuine presence, an integrated personal reality more powerful and more projected than anything else in recent books except Gary Snyder's poems about logging and fire-watching. Kinnell realizes the difference be-tween knowing something because you have been told it is so and knowing it because you have lived it. And this latter kind of knowing is what good poetry can give, and what Kinnell in some of his work gives, too. His first book is not as deep and abiding as we might like; I find myself remembering his themes and a few scattered de-tails, but not the *way* in which they are told, or, as happens with the very best poems, the *words* in which they are told. But Mr. Kinnell has made an authentic beginning, and many poets die without getting even this far. Perhaps to a degree more than is true of other poets, Kinnell's development will depend on the actual events of his life. And it is a life that I think we should watch. It is warm, generous, reflective, and friendly. And as poetry it holds out some promise, largely because of this necessary involvement with the author's life, of being in the end magnificent. It is not entirely impossible that the Wave of the Future may turn out to have begun at Avenue C, or some place within walking distance of it.

What A Kingdom It Was, by Galway Kinnell, Houghton Mifflin, 1960, $3.00.

JOHN LOGAN

In the only lines of his I have ever found memorable, Kenneth Rexroth says that the poet is "one who creates /Sacramental relationships/That last always." I have often been struck by the profundity and necessity of this statement, and I have also wondered why it is that the creation of sacramental relationships takes place so rarely in the work of most of our religious-oriented poets, men of good intent and life-long devotion to God and to writing, like Thomas Merton, Daniel Berrigan and Brother Antoninus. A sense of the sacred, which these men labor to make available, is probably the most important quality that poetry can possess, and it is not, I think, excessive to say that all poets, regardless of their orthodoxies, beliefs or unbeliefs, are trying to embody and project such a sense according to their various lights and abilities.

John Logan's approach to the problem of sacramentalism in poetry is an interesting one. To begin with, he is on the surface a very literary poet, drawing constantly on quotations from church fathers, ecclesiastical writers and also others, like Lorca and Rimbaud (you would think, from the number of poets who attach Rimbaud's words to their poems as though they were *mana*, that he made his living writing epigraphs), and in his present book not only precedes his poems with multiple quotations but also furnishes them with explanatory afterthoughts ("After Antonia Valentin and after a memorial to Heine in Kilmer Park") a practise that I simply loathe, and which I fervently wish that Logan would forget about. From a description of the subject matter of most of Logan's poems—a description citing their preoccupation with saints, with the sacred writings, with holy days, and with ecclesiastical rituals—one would be tempted to think that his approach to the creation of sacramental relationships is based exclusively upon an eminently orthodox symbology, and that it would thus run some chance of failing to convey this sense to those not of like faith and persuasion. One might conclude, also, that an habitual use of such time-worn symbols and images from an age of greater and more universally acknowledged faith would result, even at best, in a kind of museum or textbook poetry based upon matter which no amount of sincerity or ingenuity could ever restore to its former urgency. Though it is true (at least in my opinion) that his poems about saints and martyrs are not his best, the surprising thing about this part of Logan's work is that the churchly bookishness is not dry and dead; it is oddly alive and felt, for in addition to being a Catholic, Logan is a man for whom intellectual excitement exists. Even so, to a religious outsider like myself, his formidable and detailed knowledge of church history and ritual is rather forbidding, and there are a good many times when I get lost in it. If one is patient, however, one comes to see that Mr. Logan's sense of what is sacred in his own experience is by no means limited to what is officially supposed to be sacred; it does not in the least depend on his having read Saint Augustine or on any of the rest of his orthodox or unorthodox learning. His poems at their best—and Mr. Logan's work is remarkably " level," with few peaks and declines—convey to a remarkable degree that degreeless and immeasurable and unanalysable quality which Albert Schweitzer has called, in our century's greatest phrase, " reverence for life." In the face of this feeling, which is constant throughout Mr. Logan's writing, one does not really care much about talking of his literary means. His technical abilities are relatively slight, and really begin and end with an uncommon capacity for coming up with a strangely necessary and urgent observation and setting it among others by means of ordinary, unemphatic but rather breathless language which makes his lines read something like a nervous, onrushing prose. The heavy machinery of his religious symbology looks at times a little incongruous in this setting, but Logan himself never does. The day will come, I am sure, when he will lay less stress upon the symbols provided by his church, and rely more upon what he has so abundantly and joyously: the spirit of love without which all the dogma of Christianity would be valueless. I know of no other writer of my generation who so consistently is able to project this quality, and Logan does so entirely without recourse to that awful and professionally useful kind of " love " that is no more than a word on a page, and is often mistaken for the spirit that infrequently underlies it. Logan mentions love very few times in his two books, but it informs, illuminates and transfigures everything he writes about. One closes Logan's books—particularly the present one, markedly superior to the first—thinking, "Yes, this is what poetry can sometimes do; this is what it can sometimes be." One understands what the religious faculty in man really is, and the human miracles it can perform even in its impure modern environment.

Mr. Logan's poems have not, perhaps fortunately, been widely or well reviewed; perhaps they could not have been. His strange kind of innocence, walking in and out of his ecclesiastical and literary knowledgeableness, is not an easy thing to talk about, though anyone who reads Mr. Logan cannot fail to be excited and uplifted by it. He is very much out of place, too, in the pathetic and vicious jostling and literary back-scratching for prizes and favorable notices that shows his generation of American poets at its ineffectual worst. He is far beyond the Idols of the Marketplace, and works where the work itself is done out of regard for the world he lives in and the people he lives among because he is helplessly and joyously what he is. As (and if), in Logan's work, the letter of religion fades away in favor of its spirit, he stands, in my opinion, an exciting chance of being one of the finest poets we have ever had in this country. (It might help, also, if he could find a less prosaic way of writing, and if he would explore a little among the dynamics of language, always retreating when they became too interesting for their own sake). It might be given to Logan to show in exultant urgency and truth what so many have labored and failed to show, but only said: that the spirit that makes Christianity Western Man's greatest triumph and hope is always and perpetually available in everything the human creature is privileged to do, from bringing children to birth to caressing the head of a dog.

Ghosts of the Heart, by John Logan, University of Chicago Press, 1960, $2.75.

W. S. MERWIN

W. S. Merwin is probably the most widely published poet of his generation. That he is a fine writer I have no doubt at all, and that in his new book he displays signs of a power I had not hitherto noticed is equally true. Even at his most ornamental he has never been near the obvious and busy emptiness of so many other American poets his age, though one has certainly remarked the low-keyed monotony of some of his descriptive poems and the endless fascination that the mechanical problems of writing verse have always had for him. What he has lacked up to now, and still lacks, is intensity, some vital ingress into the *event* of the poem which would cause him to lose his way among the intricacies of what is so easy for him to say concerning almost anything on earth and suffer a little at the hands of his subjects: in a word, *earn* them emotionally. Control of one's material is one thing, and dictatorship over it is another. It is this, I suppose, that led " Crunk," the critic of the *The Sixties,* to speak of Merwin as being " like a great general born into the world again as a member of the animal kingdom." It seems to me, also, that Merwin has never given enough of himself to his subjects: of the self that somehow lies beyond the writing self. He has always seemed so sure, so utterly sure of the things he knew and what he could tell about them that the strokes out of Heaven, or out of the subjects themselves, have never quite managed to hit him between the eyes. One of the difficulties about Mr. Merwin's writing generation has always been just this, as I have noted before: the dominations and powers of poetry itself—of the surface effects and the learnable manipulations as opposed to the profound marriages of technique and personality that make up the poems we remember—are constantly in danger of becoming a kind of mask which takes, automatically, a more or less pleasing, predictable shape, but which also with tremendous effectiveness obscures and kills what the poet should want to get at: those areas which only he is capable of discovering. In a land where all poems are masks, good ones or bad ones, it behooves the poet to construct the best faces for himself that he can. And yet when the right kind of simplicity reveals itself, how artificial all such construction and its products come to seem!

I think that his own kind of simplicity is now becoming available to Merwin, and the fact that it is slowly emerging from the techniques of one of the master prosodists of our time makes its advent doubly worth watching. There is still far too much gilded stuffing rounding out the contours of Mr. Merwin's poems, and I can't yet see his features clearly through his various masks, but I hope that one day in the not-too-distant future I shall be able to do so. After a prodigal beginning Merwin may now seem to be stalled. But it is my impression that he is gathering force. The title poem here and " One-Eye " avail themselves of an odd kind of roughed-up, clunking diction and meter that I found quite attractive, and which involved me in their poems more than in any of Mr. Merwin's others that I have read. With tools like these and with the discoveries about himself that this book shows him intent on making, Merwin should soar like a phoenix out of the neat ashes of his early work.

The Drunk In The Furnace, by W. S. Merwin, Macmillan, 1960, $1.25.

WILLIAM STAFFORD

There are poets who pour out rivers of ink, all on good poems. William Stafford is one of these. He has been called America's most prolific poet, and I have no doubt that he is. He turns out so much verse not because he is glib and empty, but because he is a real poet, a born poet, and communicating in lines and images is not only the best way for him to get things said; it is the easiest. His natural mode of speech is a gentle, mystical, half-mocking and highly personal daydreaming about the landscape of the western United States. Everything in this world is available to Mr. Stafford's way of writing, and I for one am very glad it is. The things he chooses to write about —I almost said " talk "—seem in the beginning more or less arbitrary, but in the end never so. They are caught up so genuinely and intimately in his characteristic way of looking, feeling, and expressing that they emerge as fresh, glowing creations; they *all* do, and that is the surprising and lovely fact about them:

> The well rising without sound,
> The spring on a hillside,
> The ploughshare brimming through deep ground
> Everywhere in the field—
>
> The sharp swallows in their swerve
> Flaring and hesitating
> Hunting for the final curve
> Coming closer and closer—
>
> The swallow heart from wing beat to wing beat
> Counselling decision, decision:
> Thunderous examples. I place my feet
> With care in such a world.

Let Mr. Stafford keep pouring it out.   It is all good, all to his purpose.

A characteristic Stafford poem makes itself felt with soft, delicate insistence; one somehow becomes stiller on reading it, convinced from the first few words that one must miss nothing of what is being so quietly and confidently said :

> On the third finger of my left hand
> under the bank of the Ninnescah
> a muskrat whirled and bit to the bone.
> The mangled hand made the water red.
>
> That was something the ocean would remember :
> I saw me in the current flowing through the land,
> rolling, touching roots, the world incarnadined,
> and the river richer by a kind of marriage.
>
> While in the woods an owl started quavering
> with drops like tears I raised my arm.
> Under the bank a muskrat was trembling
> with meaning my hand would wear forever.
>
> In that river my blood flowed on.

West of Your City, by William Stafford, The Talisman Press, 1960, $5.00 (cloth), $2.50 (paper).

DAVID IGNATOW

I—The Gentle Weightlifter

David Ignatow writes a flat near-prose which sometimes
helps his poems toward the kind of innocence and legend-
ary strangeness they try for. The ultimate effect of its
use, however, is numbing. Through repetition, under-
statement loses the sense of the deliberately left-out or
held-down that should enhance the suggestiveness of the
individual poem, and the poems tend to blur and run
together.

The best pieces in *The Gentle Weightlifter* might be
called " Secret Histories." Oedipus, Aeneas, Achilles,
King David are seen moving confidently and unsuspecting-
ly through their familiar roles, to become resigned and
incredulous at the end-results. The reader, too, thinks,
" Why, anyone could have made that mistake, and now
look what's come of it."   The perfectly human actions of
these people have somehow been chosen to become fabul-
ized and " illustrative," but Ignatow's interest and sympathy lie with the human beings who must, unknowingly,
act out the myths, and suffer as men their final point. His
is a kind of parable-poetry, emphasizing the individual act
and its effect on the participant rather than the general-
izing or transcendent power of the episode.

> At Colonnus Oedipus complained;
> Antigone attended him.   He thought
> The sun too hot, she shielded him;
> His enemies too strong, she fought
> For him; his life bitter, she soothed him;
> And hope gone, like all things.
> His blinded eyes pained him, she bathed them;
> And when he left, by decree forced to,

She went with him, her arm supporting him;
And where he lay at the end of his strength,
Stretched out upon the forest floor,
His head pillowed in her lap,
His arms at his sides trembling,
She thought surely some cover
Could be found for him.

Aside from the flatness, which is only in a very rudi-
mentary sense a technique, Ignatow does almost completely without the traditional skills of English versifica-
tion. He makes no effort to assure his lines rhetorical
effectiveness; the import of each poem is thus far too
dependent upon *what* is said, given in a low, gentle, spell-
breaking murmur. At his best, however, Ignatow often
seems a real primitive, with the small, serene vision of the
Douanier Rousseau or of Bombois. His narrative gift
appears to me to be worthy of encouragement, and I look
forward, queerly, since concision and concentration are
integral to Mr. Ignatow's successes here, to longer work.

The Gentle Weightlifter, by David Ignatow, The Morris Gallery,
1955, $3.00.

II—*Say Pardon*

David Ignatow is in a strange and necessary category;
his own. I have liked his work for a very long time, ever
since his *Gentle Weightlifter*, and have watched the poems
in the present book come out in various places with the
growing conviction that they would make a superb showing when they were collected. They do. This is one of
the three or four best books—with James Wright's *Saint
Judas*, Robert Francis' *The Orb Weaver* and Louis Simpson's *A Dream of Governors*—that Wesleyan has brought

out, and these four titles alone give that house the most exciting poetry list in current American publishing. Ignatow's poems are in no sense inferior to the best of Wright's or Francis's, which is to say that they rank with the most authentic now being written. What gives them their unique power is a kind of strange, myth-dreaming vision of modern city life, and the ability to infuse the decor of the contemporary city with the ageless Old-Testament fatality of death and judgment: to make the traditional moral issues of the race count in an environment where seemingly they have ceased to, and to give them a fitting dramaturgy of symbol and image which not only brings the reader into the situations Ignatow writes about, but makes him subject to the same unchangeable laws: judges him, doesn't let him get away untouched. There is no obvious brilliance of language such as the academic poet is straining to achieve; in Mr. Ignatow's use, words are merely a vehicle for recounting what happened: what happens. The dramatic impact of each poem hits you foursquare, always convincingly, and the whole thing, the incident, the judgment, is what you remember. Mr. Ignatow's is a " total poetry " in a different sense from that in which the term is ordinarily used; not like that, say, of Hopkins or Dylan Thomas or Mallarmé. Rather than being word-oriented, it is an inspired and brilliantly successful metaphysical reportage, with an " I-was-the-man " authority that shakes the involved beholder to his bones.

> Someone approaches to say his life is ruined
> And to fall down at your feet
> And pound his head upon the sidewalk.
> Blood spreads in a puddle.
> And you, in a weak voice, plead
> With those nearby for help;

Your life takes on his desperation.
He keeps pounding his head.
It is you who are fated;
And you fall down beside him.
It is then you are awakened,
The body gone, the blood washed from the ground,
The stores lit up with their goods.

Say Pardon, by David Ignatow, Wesleyan University Press, 1960, $1.25.

TOWARD A SOLITARY JOY

The battles of art are silent, bloodless, and usually result in defeats more total than any others. This is especially true of poetry, where the writer has virtually no audience at all, and puts in his hours, almost always after work, in dogged misery, determined to realize himself and to communicate even if there is no one to communicate with. It is heartbreaking, truly. And yet, like everything else, it has its good side. Nothing else on earth can equal the profound and upsurging sense of personal justification that a good line or a good poem gives one, and, in the dead quiet after midnight or the groggy dawn when the poet seizes whatever time he can to get that new, promising poem together, he can be assured that this feeling will come again, maybe tomorrow, maybe next month, maybe next year, if he sticks at it. The carping of critics matters very little beside this, though critics are doubtless bothersome enough, for the poet's " place in the literature of his time," his place in the anthologies and textbooks that are his only Valhalla, are largely determined by what people, professionally knowledgeable people, think and say about him in public. Yet literary vanity disappears in the light of the truly creative moment; the hardscrabble labour of writing poems is quite literally its own reward. The major good of writing a poem is done to the poet, and if a faint radiation of this central good gets as far away as somebody else, that is extra. But nobody can really count on it. Therefore, without being asked, I encourage all bad poets as well as good ones to write, and for the rest of their lives, for whatever is in it for them. My comments, such as they are, can't touch *them*, really, and I only offer what seems to be reasonable advice to help some of them toward that lonely, unfathomable rising of joy between teaching Chaucer and freshman composition, or at night after grading papers, or on the commuter train to Scarsdale.

Why, indeed, do people write poetry? Especially, why do increasing numbers of them write it now, in an age wherein poetry is supposed to be kicking weakly in its final throes? For every poem in these books there must be thousands and thousands in manuscript, written by housewives, teachers, school-children, porters, clerks, secretaries, advertising executives (even), lawyers, salesmen. Why? All of these poems, one imagines, come out of the unconscious conviction that significant emotions must, somehow, not be lost, and that they surely will be, if action of a kind is not taken. Almost everyone believes that at least a few moments of his life belong uniquely to *him;* that these, in fact, *explain* his life, and must be protected from or made to stand against the monstrous manipulation of human interests for gain; the treatment of humanity as " the consumer," and the terrible attendant rationalizations by the Powers that have it so (" But we're helping them get what they want!") The least of these poets, the most unschooled and desperate, have nothing to do but moan or howl. A few cuts above these are the writers who have dimly sensed that Form has something to do with the quality and the communicability of what they wish to say. These are beginning the essential journey, though as poets they die by thousands along the way, many of them after taking no more than a step or two. A third group—the artisans—are consciously seeking all their lives to forge the great key of a style, and, if successful, to employ it as extensively and wisely as possible. Though a few of the poets here discussed have entered the City of Artisans, none has stood in the " artifice of eternity " with Yeats, or made or become the golden singing bird. Lacking greatness, however, there is much variety here: strong dedication, devotion to a

119

medium and, one must conclude, love. To read even a dreadful poet like Tennessee Williams after watching an evening of give-away programs and "true-life dramas" on television, or looking with half-persuaded and fascinated disgust at the rest of the comfortable and deadening "Consumer's Paradise" around us, where every means is used to persuade us that life, American life, consists, doesn't it, of the radiant happiness of the clean, pretty, harmless, and helpful things we buy, and of the nice, fun-loving people that we ourselves should (no; *must*) want to be: to read even Williams, or Allen Ginsberg, is to have one's eyes fill with tears. At times the hardest of the reviewer's tasks is to keep himself from saying to his little stable of poets, regardless of his likes and dislikes: " Yes! Yes! Go on and do what you're doing: write. You're all wonderful! You've declared in favor of humanity, and that fact itself must endear even your faults to anyone who sees what you are trying to preserve. I take your hands! I bless you all!" It is with the cold knowledge that he would, by such an attitude, be depriving the writers of whatever small help (perhaps none) he could be to them, in their effort to belong to " the opening world," to move among the vital potentialities of life and proclaim them, that the critic sinks back with a sigh on his own opinions, and takes up again the hard and frequently bitter business of discrimination, which is not the wildness but the practicality of hope. The sworn enemy of such hope is the Suspect, who, like the Devil, is always with us. And, like the Devil, he (or it) is infinitely various, and can take every form but God's. For every reader there are poems to which he responds with no prompting from criticism or from his tutored, knowledgeable self. Let us cleave hard to those, and, because they betray nothing, neither us nor the world nor their poets, let us be doubly ruthless to the Suspect, and deny him whenever he may arise, offering us a synthetic apple.